P9-ARX-355

**NEW DIRECTIONS
FOR STUDENT
SERVICES**

Number 13 • 1981

NEW DIRECTIONS
FOR STUDENT
SERVICES

A Quarterly Sourcebook
Ursula Delworth and Gary R. Hanson, Editors-in-Chief

Number 13, 1981

Increasing the Educational Role of Residence Halls

Gregory S. Blimling
John H. Schuh
Guest Editors

Jossey-Bass Inc., Publishers
San Francisco • Washington • London

INCREASING THE EDUCATIONAL ROLE OF RESIDENCE HALLS
New Directions for Student Services
Number 13, 1981
  Gregory S. Blimling, John H. Schuh, Guest Editors

Copyright © 1981 by Jossey-Bass Inc., Publishers
                and
            Jossey-Bass Limited

Copyright under International, Pan American, and Universal
Copyright Conventions. All rights reserved. No part of
this issue may be reproduced in any form—except for brief
quotation (not to exceed 500 words) in a review or professional
work—without permission in writing from the publishers.

New Directions for Student Services (publication number
USPS 449-070) is published quarterly by Jossey-Bass Inc., Publishers.
Subscriptions are available at the regular rate for institutions,
libraries, and agencies of $30 for one year. Individuals may
subscribe at the special professional rate of $18 for one year.

Correspondence:
Subscriptions, single-issue orders, change of address notices,
undelivered copies, and other correspondence should be sent to
New Directions Subscriptions, Jossey-Bass Inc., Publishers,
433 California Street, San Francisco, California 94104.

Editorial correspondence should be sent to the Editors-in-Chief,
Ursula Delworth, University Counseling Service, Iowa
Memorial Union, University of Iowa, Iowa City, Iowa 52242
or Gary R. Hanson, Office of the Dean of Students,
Student Services Building, Room 101, University of Texas
at Austin, Austin, Texas 78712.

Library of Congress Catalogue Card Number LC 80-84300

International Standard Serial Number ISSN 0164-7970

International Standard Book Number ISBN 87589-861-0

Cover design by Willi Baum

Manufactured in the United States of America

378.1987
I37

83-5452

Contents

Editors' Notes   Gregory S. Blimling   **vii**
                                            John H. Schuh

Residence Halls in Today's   Gregory S. Blimling   **1**
Compartmentalized University

> In the educational setting, residence halls are viewed as supplemental to
> the educational process. In the 1980s residence hall educators must dem-
> onstrate that this experience is central to the educational development of
> students.

A Philosophy of Community   Thomas J. Hennessy   **13**
Development for Residence Halls

> Residence hall programs should exist for the primary purpose of educat-
> ing students. This chapter states a philosophy for working with students
> in residence halls and clarifies the educational foundations of residence
> halls.

Educational Programming   Fred Leafgren   **23**

> Residence hall professionals teach through educational programming.
> Both the process and function further the educational aims of residence
> halls.

Student Development Through   Charles C. Schroeder   **35**
Environmental Management

> The residence hall environment should be adapted to meet the develop-
> mental needs of students.

Environmental Structuring: Linda Pedretty Rowe   **51**
Residence Halls as Living
Learning Centers

> The key elements of designing a residential environment that maximizes
> learning are examined.

Selecting Competent Residence   D. David Ostroth   **65**
Hall Staff

> Both professional staff and undergraduate staff serve as educators in
> residence halls. Wise staff selection is essential.

Staff Training   John H. Schuh   **81**

> If staff are to implement the educational program and accept a united
> educational philosophy for working with students, they must have the
> necessary resources, skills, and educational background. This chapter
> discusses these training needs.

Influences, Predictions,   Gregory S. Blimling   **95**
and Recommendations   John H. Schuh

In this final chapter, the editors examine the major influences on residence halls, predict some of their effects, and recommend some preparations for the future.

Annotated References   Janice L. Diehl   **103**

Some selected resources for further reading are listed.

Index   **111**

Editors' Notes

In the last three decades, residence hall programs have experienced a variety of significant developments, which have not always complemented one another. The 1950s were characterized by the emergence of professionally trained individuals to plan, supervise, and conduct residence hall programs. The role of these new professionals was significantly different from the functions of the former housemothers, graduate students, or others, who were warm, caring people but who had little understanding of the growth and development students could undergo in a residential setting. The following decade, the 1960s, was clearly a time when the reins of parietal control were loosened. Students fled campus residence halls for the less restricted atmosphere of off-campus housing. Even though the 1960s saw many students leaving campus residence halls, the 1970s found them returning to campus residence halls in record numbers to seek an educational environment that would complement their classroom and laboratory experiences. As we move into the 1980s, it is clear that a framework must be developed to maximize the development of students in the residential setting.

The purpose of this sourcebook is to develop a framework that maximizes student growth and development in the residential setting. A variety of research studies finds educational benefits in the residential experience. The studies note that students grow at an accelerated pace while they live in residence halls. However, an important concern remains as to whether that growth is the result of intentional interventions developed to enrich the residential environment, or whether that growth is mere chance. This sourcebook focuses on specific steps that those responsible for the educational development of students in residence halls can take to ensure that student development is not a chance occurrence but a planned intervention to help students fulfill their potential for academic and personal growth.

Gregory Blimling begins the sourcebook by discussing the role of residence halls in the educational setting. He suggests that residence halls must be brought into the mainstream of the educational experience of students and cease to be viewed as supplemental or extracurricular to the activities of students.

Thomas Hennessy, in the next chapter, focuses on the philosophical background for educational development in the residence hall. He views the residential setting as a laboratory for student development and outlines a framework that brings faculty and students together to enhance the learning experience.

The application of student development concepts to residential programming is the theme of Fred Leafgren's work in the third chapter. Leafgren addresses the issues of developing a philosophical framework for educational programming, defines the various applications of educational programming, and recommends a number of programs that might be applied in the residential setting.

In the fourth chapter, which addresses the broad concept of environmental management, Charles Schroeder brings together his past research on developing the optimal residential environment. Schroeder has conducted extensive research on many theoretical topics associated with the development of residential environments, and in his chapter he applies the findings of his research to the practical residential setting.

Linda Rowe builds on the findings of Schroeder in her chapter on environmental structuring. She focuses on the development of specialized environments that promote student growth. A major theme of her work is the growth of the living learning center. Rowe recommends a series of steps to develop this unique residential environment.

An essential ingredient in the development of the residential environment is the residence life staff. In the next chapter David Ostroth addresses the problems and dynamics involved in the selection of a strong staff. He discusses the criteria for selecting professional and student staff and the process by which the staff might be selected.

In the seventh chapter John Schuh attempts a systematic, comprehensive approach to staff training. He believes staff trainers should use a sequential framework that employs skills developed in one phase of training as the basis for training in the next.

In the final chapter, John Schuh and Gregory Blimling identify the major influences on higher education, make some predictions about the effect of these influences on residence halls, and use information from other sourcebook contributors to make some recommendations for the future. Janice Diehl prepared the annotated references, which refer the interested reader to resource materials that give further information on the topics addressed in this sourcebook.

When the idea for this sourcebook was germinated, Dr. Elizabeth Greenleaf agreed to assume a significant responsibility for its development. However, her untimely death made that involvement impossible. Betty Greenleaf played a significant role in the development of residence halls programs over the past three decades and was a cherished mentor and colleague of the editors. This sourcebook is dedicated to her memory.

Gregory S. Blimling
John H. Schuh
Guest Editors

Gregory S. Blimling is associate dean of students at Louisiana State University, Baton Rouge.

John H. Schuh is director, Department of Residence Life at Indiana University, Bloomington.

To meet our responsibility for educating the whole person within today's
compartmentalized university, we must make providing a total
educational experience central to the mission of the university.

Residence Halls in Today's Compartmentalized University

Gregory S. Blimling

Higher education has been described variously as an organized anarchy (Cohen and March, 1976), a system of pressure influences (Stern, 1964), and a collection of relatively autonomous professional schools and specialized departments (McConnel, 1976). In recent years the once exalted ideal of a university community has not existed in a meaningful way in any but the small liberal arts college. Every year higher education is moving further from this ideal. In this chapter we examine the emergence of compartmentalization, the effect it has had upon the ability of universities to develop the total person, and the role played by residence halls in offering an important vehicle for realizing the total development of the student in today's universities.

The Emergence of Compartmentalization

Increased enrollments are most often blamed for the decline of the university community. As more students entered higher education — an increase from six hundred thousand to over fifteen million in the past sixty years (National Center for Education Statistics, 1979) — the frequency of personal contact between faculty and students and among students diminished. The GI Bill, the National Defense Student Loan program, special programs for minority applicants, and other special government subsidies changed the homogeneous blend of faculty and students that characterized the university as a community. Common values and experiences of the elite social strata, from which both faculty and students came, permeated this community. As universities became larger and more egalitarian, these commonalities were gradually lost.

However, increased enrollment is not the whole story. Of equal importance was the change in the reward system for faculty. Tenure, promotion, high salary, and colleague recognition were awarded for publishing research and securing federal grant money and not for assisting students with their personal development. Two events entrenched this trend: The federal government, perceiving the *Sputnik* satellite as a threat to U.S. technological superiority, increased subsidies to education; and private industry, hoping to recruit highly skilled people from universities, poured money into education. Higher education was called upon to do more research and train more people to compete in the race for technological superiority.

As universities grew and became more egalitarian and more research oriented, they became more compartmentalized. Each department soon had its own academic and physical (building or laboratory) territory. Because faculty contact with students was limited to in-class experiences and because faculty became more specialized, faculty lost sight of students as individuals within the context of their education and instead concentrated only on the intellectual development of students within their narrow areas of academic specialization.

This compartmentalized view, which calls upon further specialization and defines education as a trained mind, has brought about survivalist philosophy and an insensitivity toward the affective needs of students. Higher education is based upon the faculty's concept of knowledge (Katz, 1972) and is "designed *by* people who are good at academic tasks *for* people who are good at academic tasks" (Cross, 1972, p. 52). The compartmentalized view has resulted in increased competition among students and among faculty and in the revival of elite campus groups (Simon, 1980).

Higher education has all but abandoned responsibility for moral, ethical, or emotional development in favor of admission standards based on cognitive evaluation, graduation requirements based on cognitive preparation, and almost a nineteenth-century German view that faculty have no responsibility for the affective development of the student. It is the "separation of warm emotion and cool intellect [that] is the great moral tragedy" (Dewey, 1922, p. 258).

It is clear that one cannot evaluate the characteristics of an educated person simply by assessing that person's cognitive development. A person is a complex interrelationship of experience, psychological and physiological maturation, environment, and personality. To focus on only one dimension of the person—the mind—is like teaching people to swim by having them read books. The book trains the mind but not the body. "Man is not part mind and part body in the sense that a centaur is half man and half horse . . . the significant thing in the situation is the whole organism and not the parts of which it is composed" (Armentrout, 1979, p. 362).

Universities hold a public trust to develop a whole person (Truitt, 1961; Holbrook, 1980) capable of making a positive contribution to the human community. It is on this principle that a democratic society rests. We can no longer permit students to graduate from college with only the most basic skills—without having developed themselves as persons.

Feldman and Newcomb (1969) found that the primary effect of college on students' personal development is accentuating the characteristics that they bring with them to college. Yet higher education stands by as its graduates continue to be over represented among those who are divorced, who have mental health problems, who commit suicide, who are alcoholics, and who are white-collar criminals (*American Statistical Index*, 1980; *Statistical Reference Index*, 1980). The social benefit of higher education is diminishing. What we are doing is training, as one might train a child to recite the alphabet without also teaching that child to put it to use. Though higher education is not solely responsible, it must accept partial responsibility for the moral state of the nation.

Universities must be about more than information giving. Education must be about teaching both how to live and how to make a living. It must be concerned with the total development of the individual. For this to happen, universities must stop writing mission statements as descriptions of what they do and start writing them as descriptions of what qualities and characteristics they are trying to develop in students. The real concern of education should be not what universities do, but rather how much value the university experience adds to a person's life.

Four Outcomes in Defining the Educated Person

Each institution must decide what education outcomes it wishes for its students, but four basic outcomes or areas suggest themselves if an institution's goal is not simply to train a mind but to integrate cognitive and affective aspects of the individual in one educated person.

First among these areas are the qualities that will lead to a meaningful, enriched, and fulfilling life. Qualities such as "flexibility, creativity, openness to experience, and responsibility" (Sanford, 1967, p. 9) and "tolerance, interpersonal sensitivity, and personal integrity" (Cross, 1980, p. 2) must be integrated into the collegiate experience in a meaningful way. The development of these qualities should parallel the maturational development of students and draw a "purposeful relationship between formal learning and the student's growth outside the classroom" (Miller and Prince, 1976, p. 111). William Cory (1861, p. 208), a great Eton master of the nineteenth century, thought these qualities revealed themselves in "the art of expression, . . . the habit of working out what is possible in a given time, . . . [in] taste, . . . discrimination, . . . mental soberness. . . . [and] self-knowledge."

A second area of outcomes concerns the moral development of the student. Higher education has always had this responsibility, even though in recent years it has chosen to neglect it by equating it with a philosophy of "in loco parentis" or with some religious ideology. Neither is the case. The moral characteristics of an educated person transcend religion, and the responsibility to teach these characteristics in a university is basic to an educated society. As Buber (1946, p. 14) expressed it, "genuine education of character is genuine education for community."

If it is the method and not the content that is the message in teaching (Montagu, 1958), one cannot help wonder what our institutions are teaching when companies that write term papers for students flourish, property damage on campuses—and especially in the residence halls—abounds, and academic cheating in all forms is common. How many students are learning dishonesty, deceit, and complacency in place of honesty, integrity, and productivity?

Stamatakos and Stamatakos (1980), in a discussion of the need for universities to return attention to the moral development of students, see new values, pragmatism, and apathy as examples of conditions that emphasize this need. They write, "Expedient and insidious competitiveness, rampant privatism called 'personal freedom,' increased tolerance for all but the most heinous felonies, and a big splash of hendonism [sic] have replaced the colleges' traditional moralism" (p. 58). Clearly, the development of a moral person is a legitimate mission of the university and a necessary outcome in developing the educated person.

The next area of outcomes should focus on preparing students to meet future demands. Universities should strive to foster in the student the ability to make decisions, assume responsibility, and work as a team member (Truitt, 1961). The student should be "developing qualities and abilities to deal with [the] job years down the road much like West Point trains people to become generals, and not lieutenants" (Cardozier, 1979, p. 479).

Finally, we should instill students with the desire for continued learning. Too many students believe that upon graduation they have been educated (St. Clair, 1979) and close their minds to further learning. If the objective is to create an educated person, universities should graduate people who continue to learn and seek new knowledge. "Teach a man to read and write," wrote Huxley ([1868], 1971, p. 85) "and you have put in his hands the keys to the wisdom box. But it is quite another matter whether he ever opens the box or not."

It is in these four areas—(1) instilling qualities that lead to a fulfilling life, (2) developing in students a sense of moral integrity, (3) providing students with the skills necessary to meet future demands, and (4) creating in students the desire to learn—that universities should look when they describe the outcomes they wish for their students.

A Dualistic System of Education

It is unrealistic to expect the faculty to move outside of the classroom to help the student develop outcomes beyond cognitive abilities, especially in light of shrinking federal grant money, gradually declining enrollments, increased student credit hour formulas dictating larger classes, diminishing job security, and growing pressure to publish. It is fruitless to lament that faculty should be doing more for the students' total development. The reality is that in all probability this situation will not change. Faculty members will continue to perpetuate their academic specialities; and universities, in the coming years of fiscal austerity, will continue to maintain student credit hour formulas based on balancing the budget. The concept of community is no longer a viable model in the compartmentalized university of today. It has been replaced by a cognitive-affective dualistic system (Cross, 1980) that relegates to the faculty the cognitive development of the student and everything else to student development staff. Though one can argue convincingly for joining these two aspects of the students' learning through a rebirth of the community in the university, such a union, though desirable, is unlikely.

The success of this dualistic system in producing the educated person depends on the ability of student development professionals to guide the emotional, maturational, and personal development of students and the ability of faculty to guide the intellectual development of students. This is not to imply that we can proceed with the affective aspects of a person's development without regard for the person's cognitive development, as has been the case in reverse, or that this development can take place in a vacuum in the absence of the faculty. The development of the educated person cannot be brought about by either of us excluding the other. "Education is, or should be, a cooperative enterprise, beyond all else an undertaking in the learning of the theory (that is, the science) and the practice (that is, the art) of human life" (Montagu, 1958, p. 150). One function is not more important than the other. The functions are joined and are therefore complementary.

Our best efforts at this development have been made through the educational experience of the residence halls. We must be successful in the residential setting where our influence is greatest, for we have fewer opportunities elsewhere. Residence halls epitomize both what is good and what is bad about student personnel. Both good and bad aspects are magnified by the control we have of the living environment. From antiquated curfew hours for female students to the massive impersonal highrise dormitories, from the living and learning centers to the intentional democratic communities, our successes and failures are graphically portrayed in the application of student personnel philosophy and institutional policy within residence halls across the country.

Though we have made strides within the past decade, we have not met fully the challenge of our responsibilities in developing the educated person. The primary reason we have not is the subordinate role assigned to the noncognitive aspects of a person's learning. This subordinate role is the result of the compartmentalization of the university and the faculty's definition of knowledge. An equally cogent reason is that our function is viewed as secondary to the mission of the university as it is now defined. And, we have done much to earn this second-class citizenship in higher education.

Examine the history of residence halls and you find they grew out of a desire to control the behavior of students (Cowley, 1934). Only within the past decade have the last vestiges of this custodial care philosophy been swept from the residence halls, and then only after a number of court decisions, the application of Title IX legislation, and the student revolts of the late 1960s and early 1970s.

We hired architects to build inverted shoe boxes of steel and glass adorned with a few opulent lounges and constructed on a formula of so many students per square foot. Shay (1969, p. 77) described these dormitories as "gilded barracks with glamorous appurtenances . . . far less homelike than many of the halls built as WPA projects in the late 1930s," and there is little evidence that they have changed much in the interim. We welcomed students into these "megadorms" with a list of prohibitions beginning with "don't paint your room," "Don't put tape on the walls," and "Don't move the furniture," which we had conveniently bolted to the floor.

As if this were not enough, we spent the last forty years trying to decide if our function in higher education was to provide services for students, manage the affairs of students, or develop students. In the processes we acquired all manner of responsibility from operating bookstores to coordinating campus parking (the functional relationship of which still eludes me). Our willingness to accept these responsibilities, whether or not they were related to student personnel work, has perpetuated the second-class status of the profession (Tollefson, 1975).

Even our theories of student personnel work were weak — theories born at a two-day conference held in 1937 that produced a "philosophy" euphemistically called the "student personnel point of view." Recently, we developed a viable theory of student personnel, the student development model (Brown, 1972; Miller and Prince, 1976), that provides a philosophy and a clear statement of our purpose. In 1957, Stroup (1979, p. 527) said of student personnel, "Its job has hardly allowed it the ivory-tower solitude and objectivity necessary for the development of high theory. Its custodial function has been accepted by many as its prime service. Being busy in supervising the laboratory, it scarcely has had the time or energy to return to the lecture in order to discover why the laboratory is held in the first place." Perhaps the student development model will herald our return to the lecture.

Next, let us examine ourselves as professionals. For years residence halls, and for that matter many areas of student personnel, were staffed with retired military people, discarded football coaches, elderly housemothers, and random others who had what Hardee (1964) described as "scout-like" qualities. They were loyal to the institution, enforced university policy, and maintained the status quo. I was amused by Hurst's description of an incident on his campus. A faculty member who was laid off by an academic department was referred to the division of student affairs for employment because of his "good rapport" with students. Hurst writes, "I thought how absurd it would be for someone being terminated from a student affairs position to be referred to the philosophy department because [he] seemed to philosophize well. It is equally

. . . absurd to think that someone who simply has a good rapport with students is prepared to serve as a full professional in a division of student affairs. And yet [this] incident has been repeated many times over across the country."

Meeting Our Responsibility

The task of meeting our responsibility for the development of the educated person within the dualistic system of the compartmentalized university stems from humble beginnings. To meet this responsibility and make the development of the educated person central to the mission of the university, we must do four things.

First, we must increase the lateral communication among the different student personnel departments and between student personnel departments and academic departments. We are as guilty of compartmentalization as anyone; each of us marks out our own territory and zealously guards it with structure charts and job descriptions. We have all seen internal bickering in student personnel departments over whether it is the responsibility of residence halls or the "union" activities staff to do programming, and who does what kind and where.

If this territorial insulation is bad among student personnel departments, it is worse between student personnel departments and academic departments. This departmental insulation must be broken down if we are to bring about greater contact across disciplines (McConnel, 1976) and function as equals with faculty in the education of students. We must function as part of the educational process and not apart from it.

Simple efforts on our part — such as hiring social science faculty in the summer to do needed research on the development of students in the residence halls, developing faculty adviser boards for the residence halls, and making inroads to team teaching through adjunct faculty positions within academic departments for professional residence hall staff — are only a few of the ways we can begin to bridge the territorial barriers between student personnel professionals and faculty.

Second, we must provide students with a meaningful residential experience that engages them and keeps them from seeking off-campus housing after the first semester. This means we will need to abandon our custodial care attitudes about students, develop new·models for educational programming (Schuh, 1977), center our educational efforts on the development of supportive communities (Mable and others, 1977), recognize the territorial imperative of students in control of their environment (Schroeder, 1978–1979), and adopt an ecosystem model in the design and redesign of residence halls (Schuh, 1978–1979). Students must be engaged in the process of their own learning toward maturation (Miller and Prince, 1976) through interaction with peers, through educational intervention strategies and milieu management, and through learner-based instruction models. We must go beyond the concept of education in the residence halls as nothing but showing inexpensive movies, getting one or two tired professors to speak on topics with catchy titles, and hiring a handful of undergraduates with only three days of last-minute training in the fall semester as our only efforts toward promoting the education of students in residence halls.

Third, as student development educators we must state clearly what it is that we do for the development of students in residence halls, publicize it, and continue to do more research in support of it. Research on the development of students through the residence hall experience has not proliferated; the past decade has produced a meager armful of publications. Student personnel is an applied discipline and as such requires evaluation of what our efforts have produced. If it is our goal to educate students, then it follows that our research should concentrate on what we have done or are doing to further this education.

Part of stating what we do is stating what we teach and the means we use to teach it. We should be teaching the four previously stated outcomes of an educated person: imparting qualities necessary for personal growth, aiding moral development, teaching skills to meet future challenges, and creating motivation for lifelong learning. We teach these things through personal example, interaction and confrontation with students, workshops and programs (Brown, 1980), and educational intervention strategies that engage the student in the process of learning through a structuring of the proper environment.

Finally, we must prepare ourselves to accept our educational role. This means selecting professionally qualified staff to fill professional positions and purging or preparing those who are not so trained. Student personnel is full of people who take refuge in being practitioners as an excuse for not knowing what they are supposed to be doing. These people are obstacles to establishing full-scale educational programs; they retreat to the solace of administrative busywork and focus narrowly on the demand for order in the residence halls (Murphy, 1969). One of the primary problems with the profession is the lack of training found in those who represent student personnel. As Stamatakos (1980, pp. 288–289) says, "The profession's perceptions, attitudes, and behaviors do not appear to have been shaped and given direction by formal study, cognitively derived principles, philosophical considerations, and commitment, but by simple, practical, operational imperatives—imperatives which have evolved and been created by college guilds and bureaucracies and which demand and reward obedience to, and efficiency for, the institution above service and responsiveness to students."

There is no justification for a professional educator working with students in the residence halls—or in any area of student personnel for that matter—not to know and understand the basic principles of student development. The theories of students' intellectual, maturational, and emotional growth should be as familiar to the student personnel professional as algebra to a mathematician or existentialism to a philosopher. This knowledge is not signaled by the initials after a name but by a willingness to keep abreast of new developments through reading, attending workshops and conferences, and maintaining an open mind to new ideas. Riker (1980, p. 177) describes the desirable state for residence hall professionals within the context of the university in this way: "Residence educators should be recognized on campus as those members of the college or university community most knowledgeable about student attitudes and needs. They should be seen as human relations experts, with skills in resolving conflicts which involve students. Residence educators should qualify as teachers, especially in the area of experiential learning, using student residences as unique opportunities for such learning."

At the same time that we are updating our professional skills and knowledge, we must stop believing that we serve a subordinate role to the educational development of students. We must stop talking about how residence halls supplement the academic process and how our programs are extracurricular. Residence halls do not supplement the educational experience; they are part of it. Our programs are not extracurricular; they are cocurricular. The difference is not semantic but conceptual. As long as we continue to view ourselves as ancillary to the process of education and act accordingly, we shall continue to be subordinate in it. Saying that we are equal and pronouncing a few conceptual changes, as we did when we changed dormitories into residence halls, is not enough. We must develop ourselves, define our mission, quit accepting superfluous responsibilities unrelated to our educational role, document our contributions, become less compartmentalized, and develop meaningful educational programs.

Meeting our responsibility for the educational development of students will take on added importance as higher education moves from the era of high enrollments and prosperity to a time of lower enrollments and fiscal parsimony. Such a transition offers higher education the opportunity to redefine its mission and establish a new direction. Whether students will benefit from this transition, gaining the advantages of developing as total persons, will depend on universities accepting this goal as the legitimate mission of higher education and on our abilities as student development professionals to meet these responsibilities within the dualistic model of today's compartmentalized university.

References

American Statistical Reference Index, 1980. Washington, D.C.: Congressional Information Service, 1980.

Armentrout, W. "Neglected Values in Higher Education." *Journal of Higher Education,* July/August 1979, *50* (4), 361–367.

Brown, R. D. *Student Development in Tomorrow's Higher Education — A Return to the Academy.* Student Personnel Series No. 16. Washington, D.C.: American College Personnel Association, 1972.

Brown, R. D. "Student Development and the Academy: New Directions and Horizons." In D. DeCoster and P. Mable (Eds.), *Personal Education and Community Development in College Residence Halls.* Cincinnati, Ohio: American College Personnel Association, 1980.

Buber, M. "The Education of Character." In G. Grigson (Ed.), *The Mint*. London: Routledge & Kegan Paul, 1946.

Cardozier, V. "Some Perspectives on American Higher Education." *Vital Speeches of the Day*, May 15, 1979, *45* (15), 476–480.

Cohen, M., and March, G. "Leadership in Organized Anarchy." In W. Lassey and R. Fernandez (Eds.), *Leadership and Social Change*. La Jolla, Calif.: University Associate Press, 1976.

Cory, W. "Eton Reform." (1861). As cited in G. Madam, "William Cory." *The Cornhill Magazine*, July–December, 1938. (Originally published 1861).

Cowley, W. "The History of Student Residential Housing." *School and Society*, December 1, 1934, *40* (1040), 705–712; (Continued) December 8, 1934, *40* (1041), 758–764.

Cross, K. P. "New Students and New Concepts in Student Personnel Administration." *Journal of the National Association of Women Deans and Counselors*, 1972, *35*, 49–58.

Cross, K. P. "Education for Personal Development." In D. DeCoster and P. Mable (Eds.), *Personal Education and Community Development in College Residence Halls*. Cincinnati, Ohio: American College Personnel Association, 1980.

Dewey, J. *Human Nature and Conduct*. New York: Holt, Rinehart and Winston, 1922.

Feldman, K., and Newcomb, T. *The Impact of College on Students*. San Francisco: Jossey-Bass, 1969.

Hardee, M. "The Residence Hall: A Locus for Learning." Paper presented at the Research Conference on Social Science Methods and Student Residence, University of Michigan, Ann Arbor, November 28–29, 1964.

Holbrook, D. "The University Is the Ultimate Sanctuary of Freedom of Spirit." *Vital Speeches of the Day*, February 15, 1980, *46* (9), 263–265.

Hurst, J. "The Emergence of Student/Environmental Development as the Conceptual Foundation for Student Affairs and Some Implications for Large Universities." In D. Creamer (Ed.), *Student Development in Higher Education*. Cincinnati, Ohio: American College Personnel Association, 1980.

Huxley, T. "A Liberal Education." In A. Beales, A. Judges, and J. Roach (Eds.), *T. H. Huxley on Education*. London: Cambridge University Press, 1971. (Originally published 1868).

Katz, J. "The Challenge to 'Body of Knowledge' Learning from the Person-Centered Associates." A paper presented at the meeting of the American Association of Colleges, January, 1972.

Mable, P., Terry, M., and Duvall, W. "A Model of Student Development Through Community Responsibility." *Journal of College Student Personnel*, January 1977, *18* (1), 50–56.

McConnel, T. "The Function of Leadership in Academic Institutions." In W. Lassey and R. Fernandez (Eds.), *Leadership and Social Change*. La Jolla, Calif.: University Associates Press, 1976.

Miller, T., and Prince, J. *The Future of Student Affairs: A Guide to Student Development for Tomorrow's Higher Education*. San Francisco: Jossey-Bass, 1976.

Montagu, A. *Education and Human Relations*. New York: Grove Press, 1958.

Murphy, R. "Developing Educational Meaning for Residence Halls." *NASPA Journal*, October 1969, *7* (2), 61–64.

National Center for Education Statistics. *Digest of Educational Statistics 1979*. Washington, D.C.: U.S. Department of Health, Education and Welfare, January 1979.

Riker, H. "The Role of the Residence Educator." In D. DeCoster and P. Mable (Eds.), *Personal Education and Community Development in College Residence Halls*. Cincinnati, Ohio: American College Personnel Association, 1980.

St. Clair, T. "Frustration or Fulfillment?" *Vital Speeches of the Day*, September 1979, *45* (22), 688–690.

Sanford, N. *Where Colleges Fail*. San Francisco: Jossey-Bass, 1967.

Schroeder, C. "Territoriality: Conceptual and Methodological Issues for Residence

Educators." *The Journal of College and University Student Housing,* 1978–1979, *8* (2), 9–15.

Schuh, J. (Ed.). *Programming and Activities in College and University Residence Halls.* Bloomington, Ind.: Association of College and University Housing Officers, 1977.

Schuh, J. "Implementing the Ecosystem Model: Phase II." *The Journal of College and University Student Housing,* 1978–1979, *8* (2), 6–8.

Shay, J. "Freedom and Privacy in Student Residences." *NASPA Journal,* October 1969, *7* (2), 76–80.

Simon, P. "The Changing Economy and Its Effect on Services, Professionals, and Students: A Cautionary Note." In D. Creamer (Ed.), *Student Development in Higher Education.* Cincinnati, Ohio: American College Personnel Association, 1980.

Stamatakos, L. "Pre-Professional and Professional Obstacles to Student Development." In D. Creamer (Ed.), *Student Development in Higher Education.* Cincinnati, Ohio: American College Personnel Association, 1980.

Stamatakos, L., and Stamatakos, B. "The Learning of Values Through Residence Education." In D. DeCoster and P. Mable (Eds.), *Personal Education and Community Development in College Residence Halls.* Cincinnati, Ohio: American College Personnel Association, 1980.

Statistical Reference Index, 1980. Washington, D.C.: Congressional Information Service, 1980.

Stern, G. "Student Ecology and the College Environment." Paper presented at Research Conference on Social Science Methods and Student Residence, University of Michigan, Ann Arbor, November 28–29, 1964.

Stroup, H. "Theoretical Constructs in Student Personnel Work." *Journal of Higher Education,* July-August 1979, *50* (4), 526–534.

Tollefson, A. *New Approaches to College Student Development.* New York: Behavioral Publications, 1975.

Truitt, J. "The Philosophy of Student Personnel Work—A Point of View." A paper presented to Men's Division Seminar, Michigan State University, East Lansing, October 18, 1961.

*Gregory S. Blimling is the associate dean of students at Louisiana State
University, Baton Rouge. He has held various administrative positions
in residence halls and other areas of student personnel at Western Illinois
University, Bowling Green State University, and Franklin College
of Indiana.*

The quality of the interactive process is greatly enhanced by a strong sense of community.

A Philosophy of Community Development for Residence Halls

Thomas J. Hennessy

A coherent statement of philosophy for community development should acknowledge at the outset a dedication to the principles of the developmental point of view. The ultimate end of this point of view is to enable each individual to reach full potential as a functioning human being. Such a statement should advocate, as Brown (1972) has urged, full integration with the academic program. It should also emphasize the necessity to promote a synthesis or symbiotic relationship between affective and cognitive education and should avoid where possible the dysfunctional dualism mentioned by Cross (1976). A statement of philosophy also should provide a view of the manner in which development occurs and relate that view to the residential setting both with regard to structure and content. For that statement of philosophy, four general assumptions are fundamental: (1) that colleges will, in the future, consciously undertake programs of education for human development, (2) that because of its unique environmental qualities the residential setting will become a primary site for such programs, (3) that these programs will make a substantial commitment to the idea of a liberal education, and (4) that there will be a reaffirmation of the principle of the preparation of leaders and citizens for a participatory role in a democratic society.

These assumptions appear somewhat tenuous when the literature is considered. For example, Cross (1976, p. 137) comments about trends in the establishment of programs for human development and notes that "few colleges in the country have consciously undertaken such programs." The situation becomes even more tenuous when the comments of other observers of higher education are considered. Galbraith (1967, p. 138) speculates about the degree to which "the educational and scientific estate, which owes the modern expansion and eminence to the requirements of the industrial system, will identify itself with the goals of the latter." In a similar vein, he expresses concern about the eventual impact of conflicts among the scholarly disciplines, such as classics and humanities; some of the social sciences; and the scientific disciplines. More recently, Rudolph (1980, p. 18), commenting on the vital link between liberal education and national leadership, concludes that "both leadership and liberal learning are in trouble." Neither Galbraith's concern for technological influences and internecine rivalries among disciplines nor Rudolph's cryptic indictment auger well for the establishment of programs in human development.

The Community Setting an Ideal Environment

A major objective of this chapter is to advance the concept that the quality of the interactive process is greatly enhanced in situations where a strong sense of community can be engendered. The rationale that underlies such community development emerges in a discussion by Inkeles (1964, p. 69).

> The essence of community is a sense of common bond, the sharing of an identity, membership in a group holding some things, physical or spiritual, in common esteem, coupled with the acknowledgement of rights and obligations with reference to all others so identified. We may designate several types of community.
>
> A *residence community* . . . is one in which the bond which unites the members in a common habitation . . . the term *moral* or psychic community is applied to those in which the sense of membership rests on a spiritual bond involving values, origins or belief. Either type may be largely *latent*, having merely potential for common action or *active* with members interacting regularly and intensely [italics added].

The linkage between the concepts of laboratory and community is based on the interactive principle they have in common. The concept of community, however, is of a higher order and lends purpose, direction, and coherence. The greatest single challenge and opportunity for development in the residence setting is in the moral dimension, "with members," as Inkeles notes above, "interacting regularly and intensely" within this framework.

Considerable work has already been done at both the theoretical and operational levels in the area of community development in residence halls. Crookston (1974) provides valuable insight at the theoretical level while Mable, Terry, and Duvall (1977, p. 50) offer a practical model that, in their words, illustrates "a concept for understanding and carrying out student development by developing community responsibility, especially in residence hall communities where self-fullfillment and community involvement are tasks of process and growth." With some thought professionals can modify this model to suit virtually any residence hall. However, they must resist the temptation to simply superimpose a new structure on an existing one and to ignore the model's potential to generate a truly participatory form of involvement. This concept implies that the process of community building must begin with the lowest common denominator, the individual student, and move to those most proximate in the living situation. The primary topic of the initial interaction must be the nature of residents' relationship to each other. That relationship will form the basis for an expandable social contact that can be integrated with the rest of the community.

Since the environment is crucial to the interactive process, it seems appropriate to devote some discussion to its implications within the context of community. While the environment probably is not divisible in a practical sense, it can be separated arbitrarily into three parts for the purposes of this chapter: (1) the physical environment, (2) the interpersonal environment, and (3) the normative environment. These divisions derive from the general objectives of college student housing identified by Riker and DeCoster (1971); and, although they are not being used here to define functional responsibilities for management and educational personnel, they do have the same implications.

The Physical Environment. On many if not most college campuses, residence hall facilities predate student development concepts. Even after the advent of such concepts, little recognition was given to the dramatic role played by the physical environment in creating atmospheres conducive to student development. The professional literature used words such as *satisfactory* or *adequate* when referring to the physical environment and indicated only marginal appreciation of its potential impact. Writers such as Grant (1974) have begun to call attention to the relationship of the physical environment to psychological needs. He advocates developing zones or areas catering specifically to such needs as stimulation, security, and freedom. Grant also stresses the need to foster a sense of "turf" or territoriality. Somewhat later, Schroeder, Anchors, and Jackson (1978) translated these important concepts into tangible strategies for humanizing the physical environment of residence halls. In philosophical terms, the message is emphatic and simple. It is absolutely crucial that residence hall environments be humanized in every reasonable way and adapted to complement the developmental process. For those must make do with antiquated residence halls, creative management, modification, and flexibility are imperative. Those fortunate enough to have a say in planning new facilities should take care to incorporate the new concepts.

The Interpersonal Environment. The operative principle for the development of community within this context is enrichment of the environment. The concepts of responsible citizenship and regard for others need to be constantly reinforced and maintained. The primary thrust of activity in this context should be to provide opportunities for growth and development through conscious efforts to enrich the environment, thus providing an atmosphere that is not only conducive but also responsive to learning. This places a heavy premium on deliberate, planned programs for environmental enrichments. Unplanned interactions may provide indications of problems, interests, and needs, but the responses to such interaction should be carefully devised. Three basic assumptions underlie the principle of enrichment as it is conceived herein: (1) that the process of enrichment will follow developmental lines, (2) that the process will draw heavily on the humanities, and (3) that the faculty will play an integral role in the process. Each of these assumptions will be considered in turn.

First is the relation of enrichment to development, which is well documented. Perhaps the most familiar and comprehensive examination of student development at the college level is Chickering's (1969). Chickering identifies seven developmental vectors that affect college students as follows: (1) achieving competence, (2) managing emotions, (3) becoming autonomous, (4) establishing identity, (5) freeing interpersonal relationships, (6) clarifying purposes, and (7) developing integrity. The five developmental tasks identified by Coons (1974) are similar to Chickering's. Since Coons' were generated through clinical relationships with college students, they are more specific and useful. Coons identifies several developmental areas: resolving of a personal value system, developing capacity for true intimacy, and choosing a life's work. These developmental referents are presented to suggest that virtually all conscious educational efforts in the residence communities should help students with these crucial tasks.

The second assumption is that enrichment will draw heavily on the humanities. The term *humanities* as it is used here refers to such disciplines as history, literature, poetry, comparative religion, languages, and philosophy. It also implies an overlap and association with the liberal and fine arts. One reason to study humanities is to learn about the ideas of scholars and thus enrich and expand the capacity for thought. Some exposure to the cultural, intellectual, and moral traditions that are our common heritage is necessary to gain an informed view of the world. More importantly, study of the humanities helps the student to think more rigorously and develops the habit of reflection before action. This in essence means not only knowing how to do things but also considering whether or not they should be done. Increased specialization and the rising cost of credit hours have caused many students to turn away from the study of the humanities. Even on small campuses where conditions are supposed to be more favorable, Chickering (1969) found that students spent more time in rote memorization than in the exchange and refinement of ideas. The problem, as Cross (1976, p. 142) points out, is that "of giving too little attention to the education of the student as a fully functioning human being capable of using knowledge to a social end." Given the proper infusion of ideas, the residence community provides not only the opportunity for the ingestion and assimilation of ideas but also a laboratory setting in which they may be tested for validity and applicability. Ethical positions, for example, can be tested in real-life situations.

The third assumption about enrichment is that faculty participation is essential. From the developmental point of view, the compelling argument for faculty involvement arises from the need to complete the community. Residence communities as they are presently structured are almost totally isolated from adult contact. Coons (1974) points out that college students should move from the child-parent stage to the adult-adult stage of development, but with whom are they to interact? Where are the adult role models? The use of peers as staff members, excellent though it may be in other respects, is of little help in this regard. Left to their own devices, students often take as models other students no more advanced developmentally than they are. The results can be catastrophic since development is often postponed and since behavioral outcomes are frequently dysfunctional and disruptive. Riesman and Jencks (1967, p. 9) overstate the case, but there is some truth to their observation that "Feeling excluded from the world of work in which their professors participate, many students retreat to a more hedonistic world of football, fraternity parties or sex and drugs."

There are a great many more reasons for faculty to take part in the lives of students. Some of those most common are: (1) the development of a sense of total community for the institution, (2) the establishment of an academic climate, (3) the maximization of the use of resources, (4) the creation of a unity of purpose, and (5) the integration of the educational experience. These are good reasons, yet so broad it is difficult to implement programs to bring about the outcomes. There are, however, two rather compelling pragmatic reasons for faculty participation. One represents a vested interest for faculty and the other a vested interest for residence educators. First, residence communities are a superb source from which to recruit future professors. The idea that the present glut of Ph.D.'s will continue indefinitely or that the teaching profession can prosper without recruiting at least some of the best students is myopic and self-destructive. Second, faculty interaction with students is the best way to get university support for student development as residence educators perceive it. Miller and Prince (1976, p. 155) state it this way: "The institutions' commitment to student development is directly proportional to the number of these collaborative links between student affairs staff and faculty." It should be clear that this aspect of enrichment is crucial to the entire enterprise.

There is no innate polar attraction that will cause faculty and students to gravitate toward each other nor any natural alchemy that will cause them to mingle. The ideal strategy is to find some tangible reason, some common interest, to bring them together.

The emphasis on the humanities and the perceived need for faculty involvement are not intended to slight or denigrate enrichment through programs of a social and recreational nature. It should be noted that Chickering's (1969) first vector has a physical and an interpersonal dimension as well as an intellectual one. The reason for this apparent omission is that there is already demonstrated staff competence and success in the social and recreational areas of enrichment and community building. Students as well have acquired interests and skills in these areas. In fact, this fortuitous combination of circumstances sometimes give rise to a parkinsonian situation in which this dimension expands to fill the entire programmatic space.

The Normative Environment. The normative environment, as the term is used here, is defined as the climate generated through the interaction of community members and based on the behavioral standards that the community sets before itself. It is a derivative of the primary interface between the management, educational, and student structures. The fundamental dilemma of the opposition of freedom and order identified by Grant (1974) must be addressed within this context. The effects of this interaction — or lack of it — are pervasive and permeate all aspects of community life. The normative environment is, in a sense, the keystone of the environmental arch.

There are a number of prevalent myths that need to be dispelled regarding the operation of institutions of higher education impinging on the normative process. The first is the mistaken notion that colleges are utopian communities insulated from the vicissitudes that beset business and political organizations. The fact is that colleges have most of the problems that characterize other organizations and also some uniquely their own. A derivative of the utopian myth is that colleges operate on a consensual model that is essentially free of conflict. The opposite is true, as Riesman and Jencks (1967, p. 1) note: "Colleges have always been institutions that impose their values on the young." They observe that colleges, having taken on the difficult tasks of socialization ordinarily performed by parents, can hardly expect not to have conflict. The question, then, is not whether there will be conflict but how it will be managed and in what spirit. Another mistaken notion is that institutions of higher education are democracies and that students have an opportunity for an authentic experience in democratic living. At best, colleges are oligarchical arrangements with power (or more precisely authority) residing in the governing boards. They do, however, utilize democratic process. Thus though the process is democratic, the institution is not. What really is available to students is an experience in the democratic process. This experience has great value and should not be deprecated. It should, however, not be misrepresented to the community in general, and certainly not to students.

The involvement of students in the normative process is crucial. Effective involvement requires the development of a statement that defines the institutional attitude toward the students. Wagoner's (1968, p. 15) quotation of Theodore Roethke's ideas on the subject provide, with the poet's cogency and incisiveness, a statement of the problem, a suggestion for its resolution, and a rationale to support the solution. "There is an academic precept which says: Never listen to the young. The reverse should be true: Listen, I say, and listen close, for from them — if they are real and alive — may we hear, however faintly and distortedly — the true whispers from the infinite, the beckonings away from the dreadful, the gray life beating itself against the pitted concrete world."

There may be those who claim (not without some validity) that the key words here are *faintly* and *distortedly*. These are doubtless the same persons who invoke the traditional bromides to justify their lack of concern for students (lack of time, ability, and commitment) and then, after neglecting them, expect the worst from students. It behooves the educational staff in residence halls to seek the involvement of students. It is a fundamental principle of democracy that government exists with the consent and presumably the participation of the governed. This principle should provide adequate motivation. If it does not, however, a more pragmatic view may succeed where the humanistic position failed. Although students are not usually delegated much authority, they are occasionally capable of exerting considerable influence. If they are shunted out of the normative process, apathy, alienation, and disruption are likely to follow. If they are effectively involved, the result—though usually more tedious and time-consuming—is likely to be far more satisfactory.

Prerequisites for Student Involvement

There are three prerequisites to effective involvement of students: (1) an effective structure for the involvement of students, (2) the consolidation of the maximum possible amount of authority at the community level, and (3) a system of ethics to guide the process.

Structure. The structure needs to be decentralized and integrated with students, faculty, and administrative bodies at all levels. Advisory councils and committees should complement these bodies at all levels as well. Such a structure while risking some inconsistency, has the advantage of encouraging commonality of purpose and the upward flow of policy.

Authority. The authority that resides with residence hall groups is likely to be delegated and as such is subject to recall. However, this does not alter the fact that having authority and being able to fix responsibility will enhance the educational experience. Nor does it change the fact that the quality of the experience is likely to improve as a function of the amount of authority delegated.

Ethics. The development of a system of ethics is the most difficult yet most essential part of the normative process. It would obviously be impossible to develop a system of ethics for a residential community in this short chapter, but it is possible to make a few suggestions. It is essential to give immediate attention to core ethics, which, as Scriven (1965, p. 57) points out, "is that part of ethics founded upon the principle of equality of rights, the fundamental moral axiom of democracy." This principle, while widely accepted, is often misunderstood. What is most generally not understood is that those who are truly committed to equality of rights must also be committed to self-sacrifice. The idea that a stereo may be played at full volume at any time in a residence hall clearly violates the principle of equal rights and indicates a lack of understanding of its true meaning.

Extreme selfishness is often countered by extreme pluralism, which tends to immobilize students and staff. As Scriven (1965, p. 58) notes, "our allegiance to pluralism has made nonsense of our commitment to democracy." Finding the mean and maintaining it against encroachment is the prime directive of the community. As a practical matter, formal statements of ethics are available through the professional associations of both the management and educational sectors of residence halls. Some preliminary work might be done with these to make them applicable to the residence setting, at which point students might be invited to respond and to prepare a representative statement for themselves. Both the results and the accompanying dialogue should be rewarding. The ingredients are present in the residence communities to make possible experience in democratic living, but as Crookston (1974, p. 57) observes: "It takes training, hard work, practice, perseverance, responsibility and commitment to produce individuals and groups capable of self-government." Mill (1859) underscores the difficulty of developing a reasonable normative structure when he describes the difficulty of resolving the inherent conflict between collective opinion and individual independence. He concludes that rules governing such concerns should be the principal focus of society.

Criteria for Establishing Norms

It might be useful at this point to suggest some criteria for establishing norms or rules in the institutional setting. These criteria are by no means exhaustive, nor does their order necessarily reflect their relative importance.

1. *Association with the Common Good.* To be valid, institutional rules should be in the common interest. Even those rules that are completely arbitrary or based on convention may be justified as long as they serve the common purpose.

2. *Representation of Consensus.* Legal rules cease to be reasonable when they fail to demonstrate a relationship to the general view of society. In some cases rules may represent a compromise among conflicting pressures rather than consensus and should be identified as such. If the compromise is unsatisfactory, remedies should be available.

3. *Limitation in Number.* Rules should not proliferate. Rules limit those who impose them as well as those to whom they apply. Rules tend to simplify enforcement but limit the use of wisdom in treating of individual cases. These remarks should not be construed as supporting the popular fiction that the academic community could operate with no rules at all. Rather, there is an implicit suggestion that rules and sanctions play an important, if secondary, supportive role in student conduct.

4. *Adequate Promulgation.* Each individual must have a reasonable opportunity to know the rules if they are to be effective. The ancient dictum that an individual can be judged guilty of an act without knowledge or intent is still operative.

5. *Provision for Reform.* The structure needs to have within itself the mechanism for regeneration and reform. If rules conflict with the consensus or the common good or obstruct the rights of minorities, procedures must be available to resolve the conflict.

These are deceptively simple perscriptions that are often overlooked. If carefully considered and applied, they will have a salutory effect on the environment of the residential community.

References

Brown, R. D. *Student Development in Tomorrow's Higher Education—A Return to the Academy.* Student Personnel Series, No. 16. Cincinnati, Ohio: American College Personnel Association, 1972.

Chickering, A. W. *Education and Identity.* San Francisco: Jossey-Bass, 1969.

Coons, F. "The Developmental Tasks of the College Student." In D. DeCoster and P. Mable (Eds.), *Student Development and Education in College Residence Halls.* Cincinnati, Ohio: American College Personnel Association, 1974.

Crookston, B. B. "A Design for an Intentional Democratic Community." In D. DeCoster and P. Mable (Eds.), *Student Development and Education in College Residence Halls.* Cincinnati, Ohio: American College Personnel Association, 1974.

Cross, K. P. *Accent on Learning: Improving Instruction and Reshaping the Curriculum.* San Francisco: Jossey-Bass, 1976.

Galbraith, J. K. *The New Industrial State.* Boston: Houghton-Mifflin, 1967.

Grant, W. H. "Humanizing the Residence Hall Environment." In D. DeCoster and P. Mable (Eds.), *Student Development in College Residence Halls.* Cincinnati, Ohio: American College Personnel Association, 1974.

Inkeles, A. *What Is Sociology?* Englewood Cliffs, N.J.: Prentice-Hall, 1964.

Mable, P., Terry, M., and Duvall, W. J. "A Model of Student Development Through Community Responsibility." *Journal of College Student Personnel,* January 1977, *18* (1), 50–56.

Mill, J. S. *On Liberty.* London: John W. Parker and Son, 1859.

Miller, T., and Prince, J. *The Future of Student Affairs: A Guide to Student Development for Tomorrow's Higher Education.* San Francisco: Jossey-Bass, 1976.

Riesman, D., and Jencks, C. "The War Between the Generations." *The Record,* Teachers College, Columbia University, 1967, *69* (1), 1–21.

Riker, H. C., and DeCoster, D. A. "The Educational Role in College Student Housing." *Journal of College and University Student Housing,* 1971, *1* (1), 3–7.

Rudolph, F. "On Leadership and Liberal Learning." *Change,* 1980, *12* (3), 18–23.

Schroeder, C. C., Anchors, S., and Jackson, S. *Making Yourself at Home.* Washington, D.C.: American College Personnel Association, 1978.

Scriven, M. "Applied Ethics for the Campus Counselor." *Journal of the National Association of Women Deans and Counselors,* 1965, *28* (2), 57–65.

Thomas J. Hennessy is associate director, Department of Residence Life, and assistant professor (part-time) at Indiana University Bloomington. He is responsible for student development in residence halls, focusing on student government, orientation, program development, and leadership experiences for residence hall students.

A goal of educational programming is the maximum development of individuals.
Success in this goal sets into motion a process of lifelong development
that results in optimum human functioning.

Educational Programming

Fred Leafgren

Educational programming in residence halls can be readings from Milton's
Paradise Lost, which was introduced by Liberty Hyde Bailey at Cornell University before the turn of the century, or seminars on bicycle repair, which
have been introduced at many universities today. Educational programming
is not new and includes an unlimited range of topics. The goal of this chapter
is not to review the history of educational programming nor the diversity of
such programming. Its purpose is to discuss a specific form of educational programming — student development — and to discuss the implementation of student development as an educational experience facilitating change, growth,
and development in students. This chapter will examine the purpose and goals
of programming, provide a theoretical frame of reference for student development as it is applied to programming, discuss the role of staff as agents for
change, provide a model for programming, and discuss strategies for change.

Purpose of Educational Programming

Sanford (1967) identifies the terms *change, growth,* and *development* and
distinguishes three separate processes. Change embraces both growth and
development and possibly other phenomena as well. Growth, on the other
hand, is simply an expansion of the personality. He defines development as
the organization of "increasing complexity." Student development educators
are concerned with all of these processes — change, growth, and development — in college students.

Colleges and universities are agencies designed to serve functions in changing entering students. Each person's development depends on individual factors and on characteristics of the institution that he or she attends. If the university is going to be an agent of change and growth, it is important to define for students those development tasks that occur in their lives during their years at the university. We have a responsibility to let students know that we expect them to change, grow, and develop during their university years and that we have the resources to help them bring about the changes they desire. It should not be our objective to specify to students changes they must make, but rather to help them recognize the opportunities available to them, encourage their participation and involvement in programs for change, and provide programs that are effective for accomplishing these changes. The task then is one of assessing and organizing resources to achieve desired outcomes.

Institutions should help students recognize their developmental levels and then provide the means for students to bring about desired changes. According to Sanford (1967), it is the job of the institutions to present a succession of new challenges that will stimulate desired responses in the person who is changing. It is the task of the educator to find ways to reach the students, to challenge them, to jolt them out of their ruts so they will revise their ways of looking at things. Students will thus be required to generate new perspectives and systems of response. This is the purpose of educational programming.

Goal of Educational Programming

There has been considerable jargon about student development and educational programming on campuses for some time—too much jargon in fact and too few programs developed to substantiate what institutions are about. Cross (1980, p. 1) says, "Student development is a little like the weather. Everyone talks about it and is interested in it but no one does much about it." Statements about student development goals are impressive, and student development goals are often used to justify a special place in the university for student personnel professionals. But if this place is not earned by verifiable accomplishments, this justification must be abandoned. Educational programming for student development cannot be merely programming for programming's sake but must have specific goals relating to students' change, growth, and development.

The ultimate goal of student development is the optimum human functioning of the individual. Any program or experience that contributes to this goal can be considered an educational program for student development. Ideally, however, our task is identifying those programs that contribute to the greatest change, growth, and development in students.

Setting the Stage

Many students assume that if they remain in the university community long enough, they will experience the personal changes, growth, and development they seek. In other words, they expect changes in personal development to accompany intellectual growth. It is as if one stands in the rain, one can anticipate getting wet and likewise if one stays around the university, one may anticipate personal changes in life-style.

Students are not always aware that they can plan for change in the personal areas. We need to make students aware that they can bring about the changes they desire through special experiences. This point cannot be emphasized too strongly. A student can direct his or her own intellectual and personal development. Students' developmental levels can be changed by increasing their potential for optimum human functioning.

Individuals bring with them to college different degrees of readiness for change, growth, and development. Sanford (1967) makes a very significant point about this fact. He is not so much concerned with what induces effort for change as he is with the conditions and processes of change. His essential point is that a person develops by being challenged. For change to occur, there must be internal or external stimuli that upset the existing equilibrium. Lack of equilibrium causes instability that existing modes of adaptation cannot correct. These stimuli require a person to make new responses and expand the personality. Sanford maintains that it is the job of the educator to keep challenging students to grow.

Change, growth, and development occur in students when they learn new information about themselves and about choices and possibilities available to them; gain an awareness of individuality of self as well as a sense of commonality; learn a process for self-development; learn to relate past experiences to present experiences and both of these to future expectations; relate more effectively with others and to the world in which they live; and learn to utilize more effectively the personal and environmental resources available to them.

To maximize interest in change, growth, and development, we must be concerned, as Miller and Prince (1976) point out, with milieu management. The environment must be supportive. The college and university setting must offer students maximum support for undertaking change. Residence halls, with professional staffs to identify experiences and programs, can offer students this environment. If residence halls can provide significant peer support groups, a basically nonthreatening environment promoting the student's welfare, and an opportunity for the individual to identify desired areas of change, then residence halls will have provided all the elements necessary for change.

Theories of Student Development

It seems to me that the theoretical frame of reference one subscribes to is not overwhelmingly important as long as it is consistently and congruently presented to staff and students. In my experience, professional staff must understand a theoretical frame of reference that provides a way to view behavior change. This gives staff direction for their work with students and significantly increases staff effectiveness.

There is no lack of theories of personality development from which to choose. Most professionals in student personnel are familiar with Chickering's (1969) seven personality vectors of development associated with change among which are developing autonomy, developing interpersonal relationships, and developing purpose in life. Less familiar to many is the current wellness movement led by Ardell (1977), Hettler (1980b), and Travis (1977). Like Chickering's theory, this movement recognizes an optimal condition for development during the college years and has instruments designed to assess levels of wellness. Dunn (1961) defines wellness as an integrated way of functioning that maximizes the individual's ability to deal with the environment. Hettler identifies six developmental areas: the physical, social, emotional, spiritual, intellectual, and vocational, and defines what constitutes wellness in each area.

Intellectual development encourages creative, stimulating mental activities. An intellectually well person uses the resources available to expand his or her knowledge along with expanding potential for sharing with others. An intellectually well person uses the intellectual and cultural activities within and outside the classroom combined with the human and learning resources available within the university community and the larger community.

Emotional development emphasizes awareness and acceptance of one's feelings. Emotional wellness indicates the degree to which one feels positive and enthusiastic about oneself and life. It includes the capacity to appropriately control one's feelings and related behaviors including the realistic assessment of one's limitations, development of autonomy, and ability to cope effectively with stress. The emotionally well person maintains satisfying relationships with others.

Physical development encourages cardiovascular flexibility and strength and also encourages regular physical activity. Physical development increases knowledge about food and nutrition and discourages the use of tobacco, drugs, and excessive alcohol consumption. It encourages consumption and activities that contribute to high level wellness including medical self-care and appropriate use of the medical system.

Social development encourages contributing to one's human and physical environment for the common welfare of one's community. It emphasizes the interdependence with others and nature. It includes the pursuit of harmony in one's family.

Occupational development is preparing for work in which one will gain personal satisfaction and find enrichment in one's life through work. Occupational development is related to one's attitude about her or his work.

Spiritual development involves seeking meaning and purpose in human existence. It includes the development of a deep appreciation for the depth and expanse of life and natural forces that exist in the universe.

Both Chickering's vectors and Hettler's wellness dimensions provide comprehensive models for student development whose goal for educational programming is optimal, holistic, human functioning for all individuals. This is generally consistent with the overall goals of colleges and universities. Student personnel staff can further these goals through educational programming for student development. The student personnel staff must be educated in the delivery of programs that conform to one theoretical framework or another, for instance, programs that help students achieve wellness as defined by Hettler or programs based on Chickering's developmental vectors. This education, of course, is enhanced by experience and participation in educational programs for change.

Staff as Agents for Change

The preparation of professional staff to provide educational programming for student development must include study of Chickering's personality variables and Hettler's developmental dimensions. Further, the staff needs professional training in the concepts and processes of student development and its implementation.

In an interview Chickering (NASPA, 1979, p. 2) states, "I do believe student development can be effectively practiced in a large university." He further indicates that the training of people involved in student development should include a solid study of research and theory concerning life cycles in adult development and the conditions that inhibit or facilitate development. He maintains that the student affairs professional should understand the complexities of human motivation and the developmental consequences that result from interactions of different types of persons with different educational environments. As of the date of the interview, Chickering was not aware of efforts to evaluate student development programs. He prefers poorly managed programs that contain a powerful mix of ingredients for change to tidy programs that have little impact on individuals' personal lives.

Beyond the intellectual experience of learning about student development processes, student affairs professionals need to be involved in an ongoing process of development themselves (Leafgren, 1980). Facilitating development in others is enhanced by one's own involvement in developmental processes. Exposure of staff to developmental concepts and identification of their own present developmental levels and areas of desired change are essential for the staff's own change, growth, and development. The knowledge of how one changes keeps those who seek to facilitate change, growth, and development in others. This is no less true for undergraduate staff in residence halls than for professional staff. It is immensely important that these individuals also be involved in their own development.

To involve individuals in developmental programs is to have them assess their present developmental levels. This assessment can be accomplished informally through questions that enable the individuals to identify present levels of development. Two formal assessment instruments are Student Development Task Inventory (Winston, Miller, and Prince, 1979) and the Lifestyle Assessment Questionnaire (Hettler, 1980a). Whatever the form of assessment, both professional and student staff should clearly identify current levels of development on Chickering's (1969) vectors and Hettler's (1980b) six dimensions of wellness. Once these assessments are made and considered, individuals need to determine how they want their lives to change. If, as is typically the case, individuals identify more than one change, they assign priorities to the desired changes. The individuals should be encouraged to identify specific steps they will take to bring about changes in any area.

The task of student development is far too important to be approached in a random fashion. Most colleges and universities have professional staff who maintain that their major function is to facilitate students' growth and development. If this is the case, then they need to go about that task and need to go about it in effective ways. Most colleges and universities are eager to have student developmental programs. However, the vital issue is how to go about it, that is, how to implement programs.

A Model for Student Development Programming

A complete model for implementing developmental programming is presented below. This model identifies a specific set of conceptual steps to follow in implementing development programming.

1. Identify a theoretical frame of reference for developmental programming.
2. Present this theoretical frame of reference to the professional and student staff in a manner that enables them to understand the model and their role in implementing it.
3. Assess students' present levels of development in the areas addressed by the theoretical frame of reference.
4. Specify the experiences in which students may participate to change their present behavior to new developmental levels. The experiences should provide maximum opportunities for active involvement and can include programs, activities, workshops, and groups. These programs must be designed so that they specifically address the behavioral goals of the theoretical frame of reference and are catalysts for the changes desired. In other words, they must be programs specifically designed to bring about the desired behavioral changes.
5. Provide specific instructions for professional and student staff on how to use the programs developed for students. This instruction is most effective when staff participate in the programs before they use them with others.
6. Introduce the model—establishing the theoretical frame of reference, assessing present development levels, and choosing experiences designed to bring about change—to the students in clear, concise terms that result in understanding challenge.
7. The major time commitment for the professional and student staff is directing the experiences that bring about growth, behavior, and

change in students. The task of the administrative officer is to ensure sufficient staff to carry out these experiences. This may require additional staff or redesignation of present staff responsibilities to ensure that the model does not merely exist but that in fact it functions for students.

8. Implement a system to reward and recognize developmental growth in staff and students.

9. Evaluate the programs developed in terms of effectiveness with students, student interest and response, success in accomplishing the goals of the model, and practicality of the approach. Use the evaluation for ongoing program revision. This revision strengthens the model.

The individuals must be exposed to these programs, participate in them, and periodically review and assess their growth. Each individual should prepare a statement of commitment to the change, establish a deadline by which to complete the anticipated change, and set up a reward system to celebrate the changes that are accomplished.

This last point is important: individuals need to receive recognition when they accomplish desired change. A good idea is a nonacademic transcript on which to record changes and growth. In this way students' involvement in such developmental programs can become a matter of permanent record, not only for the student but also within the university community. Such a transcript can indicate specific experiences for change, growth, and development that each individual accomplishes. Moreover, the transcript can serve as a positive stimulus for involvement and change. It is a source of satisfaction for individuals to identify the changes they have created in their own lives. Brown and Citrin (1977) advocate the use of a systematic means of recording students' development through a process they call developmental transcript mentoring.

The role of student personnel professionals in facilitating change is of importance. They not only help bring about change but also teach the process necessary for change. Once students learn the process necessary for change, they can repeat the process for subsequent changes. Obviously, the experiences will differ according to the nature of the change; however, the process is the same. In each event, the process requires: a clear statement of what one wants to accomplish to bring about the change, the specific steps by which this change can be accomplished, and the assistance of professional staff in identifying the experiences and programs available to accomplish the change. Once these change steps are delineated, it is up to individuals to involve themselves in areas of experience to bring about the change.

It is important to clearly delineate the specific goal of change. In this way students will know when the change has occurred. They need to pose the question "What will be different?" at the very start so that they will know when the change has taken place. Vagueness in stating the goal and the anticipated change is most likely to lead to decreased motivation, frustration, and failure to bring about the desired change. Too frequently, goals for change are too ambitious and too vaguely formulated, and accomplishing precise changes becomes nearly impossible. For example, college students frequently want to be better liked by others. The question of how one would know if one were better liked by others immediately arises. Students must be directed to state specifically what things they want to be different and to identify how they will know when this difference has occurred. If the student responds that he or she desires more friends, then it is important that the student specify how many new friends he or she wants and what specific steps the student will undertake to make them. If the goal is to develop four new friendships during the next month, the student needs to decide several things, including steps he or she is willing to make to bring the goal about and what behavior will elicit the desired responses from intended friends.

The next major task is the development of specific programs and experiences that will result in change. The essence of educational programming is to deliver to students the skills and behaviors necessary for change, growth, and development.

Let us return to the example of the student who desires four new friendships. We could offer that student an opportunity to participate in any one of the following interpersonal relationship programs developed as strategies for change (these are only a few examples of possible programs):

- A self-awareness program exploring the basis of our best friendships
- A fantasy activity exploring desires for independence and dependence in relationships
- A movie with follow-up discussion exploring the basis of traditional roles and the implications of those roles in relationships
- A skill-based, self-awareness program exploring expectations in relationships with the opposite sex.

Strategies for Change

We are at a very exciting time in our field because we are on the threshold of becoming significant change agents. Some excellent contemporary systems—transactional analysis, gestalt therapy, rational-emotive therapy and neuro-linguistic programming—also offer strategies for significant changes in personal development and life-style. Professional staff must be trained to teach other professional staff strategies for change. All the above systems can help one facilitate change. Neuro-Linguistic Programming, the most recent system, offers some excellent strategies for bringing about change. This process, developed by Grinder and Bandler* (1976a, 1976b), utilizes strategies that can be applied effectively in educational settings. Neuro-Linguistic Programming is a model of human behavior and communication; people's internal pro-

---

*See also Bandler and Grinder (1979, 1975), Bandler, Grinder, and Satir (1976), and Grinder, DeLozier, and Bandler (1977).

cess strategies are deduced by observing their language patterns and nonverbal minimal cues. These strategies are used to elicit change through systematic communication techniques. It has been demonstrated to be a most effective and powerful vehicle for personal and social change; the theory maintains that people have all the resources to make any change they desire.

Our educational programming must be broad enough to accommodate growth in many kinds of individuals. For example, programs to assist students in accomplishing change in wellness dimensions must be sufficiently varied to address many aspects of each dimension. The programs developed at the University of Wisconsin-Stevens Point to facilitate personal growth in just one area — the physical dimension — are as follows:

Stress management	Outdoor recreation
Physical fitness	Intramural programs
Nutrition	Indoor recreation
Contraception	Body tune-up group
Blood pressure monitoring	Non-smoking group
Dental wellness	Relaxation and biofeedback training
Medical self-care	Weight lifting and exercise program
Diet education	Safety program
Nutritional menu for dining centers	Dance

Astin (1977) reports findings that students do not follow uniform patterns of development during their undergraduate years. He also indicates that although several patterns of student development are stereotypical, few students follow any given path exactly as portrayed. The patterns serve to dramatize the great behavioral and developmental differences that characterize what has come to be called the college experience.

It seems important then that the student affairs professional be highly cognizant of the need for breadth in program offerings. We need not only balanced educational programming but also varied programs to enhance the development of our many students, each of whom may be in a quite different developmental stage.

An essential element in the entire process of implementation is the assessment of programs. If we do not assess programs, we will not gain adequate knowledge about the effectiveness of our tools nor will we accomplish what we intend. Operationalizing our intentions is not adequate if we are not certain that our programs in fact accomplish our stated objectives. We must not be afraid to evaluate what we are doing. If we discover what we are doing is not relevant, then we are challenged to develop more effective procedures.

Conclusions

The heart of educational programming is to give students the skills and competencies by which and through which to change, grow, and develop. The task of educators is to develop their own competencies as change agents and to develop specific programs that teach skills for behavior change. The student affairs profession can choose from among many varied philosophical bases for student development. Means to assess development are essential. Two tasks that remain are the further development of specific experiences to change behaviors and life-styles and the thoughtful evaluation of those programs.

As student personnel professionals, we can truly be educators involved in one of the most significant of educational tasks — facilitating change, growth, and development by directing students in specific experiences, programs, and strategies. It is an exciting role. There is no more important educational programming than that directed toward student development.

What is there to gain from educational programming for student development? For all individuals involved, the increased probability of functioning at optimum level of wellness, as Dunn (1961) describes, and an integrated method of functioning oriented toward maximizing the potential of the individual in the environment. What better task could student personnel professionals be involved in than a commitment to students, their change, their growth, and their development?

References

Ardell, D. *High Level Wellness*. Emmaus, Penn.: Rodale Press, 1977.

Astin, A. *Four Critical Years: Effects of College on Beliefs, Attitudes, and Knowledge*. San Francisco: Jossey-Bass, 1977.

Bandler, R., and Grinder, J. *Patterns of the Hypnotic Techniques of Milton H. Erickson, M.D.* Vol. I. Cupertino, Calif.: Meta Publications, 1975.

Bandler, R., and Grinder, J. *Frogs into Princes*. Moab, Utah: Real People Press, 1979.

Bandler, R., Grinder, J., and Satir, V. *Changing with Families*. Palo Alto, Calif.: Science and Behavior Books, 1976.

Brown, R. D., and Citrin, R. S. "A Student Development Transcript: Assumptions, Uses, and Formats." *Journal of College Student Personnel*, 1977, *18*, 163–168.

Chickering, A. W. *Education and Identity*. San Francisco: Jossey-Bass, 1969.

Cross, K. P. "Education for Personal Development." In D. DeCoster and P. Mable (Eds.), *Personal Education and Community Development in College Residence Halls*. Cincinnati, Ohio: American College Personnel Association, 1980.

Dunn, H. *High Level Wellness*. Arlington, Va.: R. W. Betty, 1961.

Grinder, J., and Bandler, R. *The Structure of Magic I*. Palo Alto, Calif.: Science and Behavior Books, 1976a.

Grinder, J., and Bandler, R. *The Structure of Magic II*. Palo Alto, Calif.: Science and Behavior Books, 1976b.

Grinder, J., DeLozier, J., and Bandler, R. *Patterns of the Hypnotic Techniques of Milton H. Erickson, M.D.* Vol. 2. Cupertino, Calif.: Meta Publications, 1977.

Hettler, B. *Lifestyle Assessment Questionnaire*. Stevens Point: University of Wisconsin-Stevens Point Institute for Lifestyle Improvement, 1980.

Hettler, B. "Wellness Promotion on a University Campus." *Family and Community Health Promotion and Maintenance*, May 1980b, *3* (1), 77–95.

Leafgren, F. "Student Development Through Staff Development." In D. DeCoster and P. Mable (Eds.), *Personal Education and Community Development in College Residence Halls*. Cincinnati, Ohio: American College Personnel Association, 1980.

Miller, T., and Prince, J. *The Future of Student Affairs: A Guide to Student Development for Tomorrow's Higher Education.* San Francisco: Jossey-Bass, 1976.

NASPA Field Report, Fall 1979, *4* (1), 2–4.

Sanford, N. *Where Colleges Fail.* San Francisco: Jossey-Bass, 1967.

Travis, J. *Wellness Workbook.* Mill Valley, Calif.: J. Travis, 1977.

Winston, R., Miller, T., and Prince, J. *Student Development Task Inventory.* Athens, Ga.: Student Development Associates, 1979.

Fred Leafgren is assistant chancellor for Student Affairs and associate professor of Psychology at the University of Wisconsin, Stevens Point. He has made numerous presentations and consults regularly on student development, training, and wellness promotion, and he is a certified Neuro-Linguistic Programmer.

Residence educators have demonstrated only a cursory regard for the
complex interactions between students and the residence hall environment.
This imbalance in our approach to residence education has created provocative
challenges for the field.

Student Development Through Environmental Management

Charles C. Schroeder

In recent years, many student personnel professionals have reconceptualized our roles and functions. Our professional orientation has moved from controlling students, to serving students, to the current emphasis on helping students develop. With the emergence of the developmental approach, college residence hall programs across the country established new goals and priorities. In addition to the traditional emphasis on providing students with clean, attractive, and secure accommodations at the lowest possible cost, most housing programs have identified a number of objectives that include such priorities as establishing cooperative community living, developing an effective interpersonal environment, promoting academic and social competence, and providing expanded opportunities for personal growth. Residence educators have attempted to achieve these objectives by focusing their efforts almost exclusively on organizational and programmatic dimensions of the residence hall environment. They have provided a variety of life-style options, unique living learning centers, and new models for community governance — all of which have contributed to improving the quality of residence hall living for many students.

    Nonetheless, there is evidence that students continue to become disenchanted with residence hall living within a relatively short period of time (Montgomery and others, 1975). Major reasons for student dissatisfaction include lack of privacy and opportunities for solitude, inability to control personal space, roommate conflicts, forced sociability, and the absence of opportunities to personalize the institutional atmosphere (Heilweil, 1973). Most of these concerns appear to be directly related to the basic mismatch between students and the social and physical environments of their living units. Unfortunately, residence educators have demonstrated only a cursory regard for understanding and appreciating the complex interactions between students and various dimensions of the residence hall environment. This imbalance in our approach to residence education has created provocative challenges for the field. For example, in our haste to provide students with highly specialized programs and services, have we failed to identify some basic needs the students attempt to satisfy through their living environment? Have we overlooked some of the essential mechanisms of human functioning that can promote student growth and well-being? Do we really understand the effects of architectural arrangements on student behavior? Do our unsystematic, arbitrary assignment procedures create major adjustment problems for students? Finally, do we inadvertently create, through the implementation of certain administrative policies and procedures, environmental conditions that prevent us from achieving such major objectives as increasing students' satisfaction, effectiveness, and academic achievement while reducing attrition, damages, and inappropriate student behavior? Let us explore these issues through describing and analyzing the social and physical dimensions of the residence hall environment.

Two typical seventeen-year-old freshmen, Willard Wilson and Sam Hudson, arrive at Any University, USA. Everything has been done for them—they have been assigned to a nice, clean room on the fourteenth floor of the "The Towers," their residence assistant has informed them about various policies and procedures, and they are now ready to embark on their college careers.

Willard, raised in a rural community seventy miles from the nearest city, is basically an aggressive, practical, analytical type who possesses a knack for managing facts and details. Willard has already taken great pains to systematically organize his personal belongings—books are neatly arranged on the shelf, clothes are smartly hung in the closet, and his bed is routinely made each morning before he departs for class. To be sure, Willard likes to live his life according to a plan! He manages his time wisely and completes his studying promptly at 10:00 P.M. each night and then retires for a minimum of eight hours sleep. Willard reasons that since he is paying three hundred dollars per quarter in room rent, he should be able to sleep and study in a distraction-free environment. For Willard, his room is primarily a work environment—he does his socializing with one or two close friends from a neighboring residence hall.

Sam Hudson grew up in a large city of over three million. He is sociable, outgoing, warmly enthusiastic, and highly creative. Because he prefers to think about imaginative possibilities, he has real difficulty with details and always appears to be disorganized. His bed and study area are cluttered with notebooks, dirty clothing, athletic equipment, half-eaten sandwiches, and candy wrappers—in short, it appears to be pure chaos. Because of his natural tendency to work in bursts of energy, Sam's study habits are erratic. It is not unusual for him to postpone unpleasant tasks, and he may wait until the last minute to complete an assignment. Hence, he frequently pulls "all-nighters."

Sam has no trouble with distractions, and he actually prefers to study with his favorite rock music emanating from a hundred-watt, quadraphonic stereo. For Sam, his room is primarily a play environment—he enjoys socializing with a variety of people at all hours of the day and night.

It doesn't take much imagination to visualize the potential conflicts inherent in Willard and Sam's relationship. Let us examine how natural differences in basic needs, architectural arrangements, and certain administrative policies and procedures affect student satisfaction in residence halls.

Individual Differences in Basic Needs

From our description of Willard's personal characteristics, we can assume that he has a basic need for *structure*. He prefers to structure his room in ways that demonstrate order, clarity, organization, and predictability. Willard finds freedom in structure; planned, systematic ways of doing things help him feel in control, influential, unrestricted, and important. Because Willard is naturally skilled at planning and organizing things, he does not understand why Sam is so disorganized. Why doesn't Sam clean up his side of the room? Why can't Sam meet deadlines? Why doesn't Sam develop a study schedule? How can Sam study with the stereo on? Why does Sam spend so much time socializing—maybe Sam is just basically aimless and irresponsible!

From our limited knowledge of Sam, it appears that his basic needs are opposite and antagonistic to Willard's. Sam has a basic need for *freedom*. He enjoys living life in an independent, spontaneous fashion and flexibly adapts to unexpected changes in his environment. Where Willard seeks to structure and control every aspect of his environment, Sam would much rather understand than control things. In an attempt to satisfy his need for freedom, Sam avoids uninspired routines and established ways of doing things. He feels a sense of influence and control by living in accord with his spontaneous, imaginative inspirations and prefers to keep his options open by avoiding closure. Because Sam's basic needs are in opposition to those of Willard, Sam cannot understand why Willard has to organize everything or why Willard spends so much time studying. Why doesn't Willard loosen up—he always seems to have his nose to the grindstone, all work and no play! Sam reasons that maybe Willard's basic problem is that he is too rigid, inflexible, and task-oriented.

Although Willard and Sam are simply expressing their natural differences in trying to meet their conflicting needs for structure and freedom, they probably view each other as purposefully irritating. The result is often miscommunication and conflict.

Architectural Arrangements

Roommates' inability to accommodate one another's natural differences in style preferences is often accentuated by certain architectural arrangements. Small, cell-like rooms often force roommate interaction when it is not desired. The arrangement of built-in furniture may also promote undesirable confrontations. For example, students living in rooms with built-in furniture report spending less time in their rooms and using their rooms less for interpersonal recreation than students living in flexible rooms with movable furniture (High and Sundstrom, 1977).

Since most roommates expect their living areas to accommodate four basic activities—sleeping, studying, socializing, and individual relaxing—suite arrangements appear to be superior to the more traditional corridor bedrooms. Suites not only provide bedrooms that afford relative privacy for sleeping and studying, but they also provide a separate architectural space—the lounge—for socializing and relaxing. Gerst and Sweetwood (1973), comparing suite and corridor bedroom environments, found that students living in suites perceived more interaction with fellow students, more student influence, and more spontaneity—variables that were related to a feeling of happiness and contentment. It should be noted, however, that the superiority of a suite arrangement over a corridor arrangement may be evident only when the number of people on a given floor becomes too large (Baron, 1979).

Corridor arrangements, with their heavy sharing of such facilities as hallways and bathrooms, tend to increase students' feelings of crowding through too much interaction. In addition, long and narrow double-loaded hallways, with their poorly insulated walls and ceilings, and attendant noise of traffic and conversation, increased students' arousal levels. A recent study revealed that residents of long corridors were generally less satisfied with college and expressed more negative feelings toward other students and dormitory neighbors than did short corridor residents. The long-corridor residents reported that they spent less time studying and socializing in their residence hall; in addition, they reported more dormitory-related problems, described their dormitory as more crowded, and expressed greater difficulty in controlling interaction than did short-corridor residents (Baum, Aiello, and Colesnick, 1978). These findings are similar to those reported by Moos (1978), which suggest that smaller living units foster peer involvement, emotional support, and innovation. These studies imply that as group size increases, social contacts become hurried and uncontrolled; the overall environment becomes much more complex and less predictable. In such settings, students may attempt to achieve a sense of control by isolating themselves in their rooms or by spending the majority of their time away from their residence halls.

As previously stated, modern low- and highrise structures with long, narrow corridors and small, cell-like rooms tend to isolate individuals. Large lounges, designed as socializing areas, are generally geographically isolated from living areas and seldom used except for studying, an individual activity. In halls with floor lounges, the lounges are usually located at the end of corridors, remote and inaccessible from areas central to students' daily living. Unfortunately, in structures such as these, social interaction may occur more frequently in commonly shared bathrooms than in other areas.

Students' ability to achieve a balance between their needs for privacy, social interaction, and friendship formulation are not only related to size of rooms, corridor arrangements, and location of lounges, but also to the overall size of residence halls. Holahan and Wilcox (1978) found that residents of low-rise dormitories expressed significantly more satisfaction and established more residence hall friendships than students living in highrise structures. Although highrise structures appear to exert effects on students, suite arrangements seem to have compensating effects on student behavior (Valine and Baum, 1973).

Administrative Policies and Procedures

In addition to the effects of architectural arrangements, various administrative policies and procedures for decorating, maintaining, and assigning living spaces may create negative environmental conditions. Traditionally, student rooms and hallways have been painted rather bland, institutional colors. Lounges are often supplied with institutional furnishings, and it is not uncommon to find chairs and sofas arranged around the walls and bolted or chained to the floors. Such institutional decor is depersonalizing and robs the students of their identities. Excessive rules that prohibit changing the stark institutional atmosphere of rooms and hallways may cause students to feel restricted, submissive, and powerless.

Although the current emphasis in the student development field is an attempt to build a sense of community within residence halls, many residence hall staff procedures often result in student dissatisfaction and conflict. When a student like Willard Wilson is assigned to a small room with a roommate like Sam Hudson, they will find it difficult, if not impossible, to accommodate each other's natural differences and establish a meaningful relationship. Such problems are compounded by administrative practices that attempt to resolve overcrowding by tripling students. Although this procedure provides an expedient method for dealing with unanticipated overflow, it creates difficult living conditions. The results of a recent study demonstrate that residents of triple-occupancy rooms expressed greater feelings of crowding, held more negative interpersonal attitudes, perceived less control over room activities, and experienced a more negative room ambience than students living in double-occupancy accommodations (Baron, Mandel, and Griffen, 1976). When students are assigned to triple-occupancy rooms, the social environment becomes so complex and unpredictable that students devote a disproportionate amount of time and energy to negotiating the use of space. Baron and his associates indicate that in such situations students pay a high "adaptation cost" in terms of residual effects on academic functioning.

Finally, many current administrative policies present the housing profession with a rather interesting paradox. Although the student personnel philosophy has always advocated the unique needs and individuality of students, all too often residence educators have operationally assumed a "single student model" with regard to residence hall design and organizational and programmatic efforts (Titus, 1973). If residence educators want to promote greater student satisfaction and growth, they must consider all these factors: differing individual needs, impact of architectural arrangements, and effects of policies.

Given the fact that buildings already exist, students must be assigned to spaces, and everyone cannot have his or her own room, what can we do to improve residence hall conditions? Fortunately, a variety of theoretical perspectives provides suggestions that we can incorporate into strategies for change.

Theoretical Framework

Recent advances in environmental psychology offer promising theories for residence educators seeking to design new environmental management strategies. These theories are especially useful: social climate, student-environment congruency, and territoriality.

Social Climate. Moos (1976) and his Stanford associates have formulated a theory of social climate that delineates underlying patterns in various social environments. Using this theory to assess and classify dimensions of residence hall environments, Moos (1976) found that certain social climate dimensions facilitate student satisfaction, growth, and well-being. Not surprisingly, students expressed more satisfaction with residential environments that emphasized such relationship dimensions as involvement, support, genuineness, and friendship. Certain dimensions and directions of personal growth likewise tended to be associated with specific aspects of social climates. Students who lived in residences that stressed such personal development dimenmensions as competition, task orientation, and independence tended to be more productive. Too much challenge, caused overstimulation and stress, while a supporting, nonchallenging environment was seen as boring. Hence, residence educators should create designs that provide for a dynamic balance between support dimensions (relationship subsystems) and challenge dimensions (personal growth subsystems). Both theoretical and empirical support for this assertion is evidenced by such perspectives as "challenge-response" personality theory (Sanford, 1967) and "optimally incongruent environments" (Moos, 1973).

Student-Environment Congruence. Several researchers suggest that the congruence or "fit" between the type of student and the living environment may be significant for student behavior and development (Brown, 1968; Feldman and Newcomb, 1969; Holland, 1973; and Schroeder and Belmonte, 1979). For example, in our description of the difference in personal characteristics between Willard Wilson and Sam Hudson, it is apparent that their preference for such opposite and antagonistic needs as order and freedom represents a major incongruence in their relationship. In addition, certain architectural and physical design variables will also inhibit their ability to satisfy needs for privacy, social interaction, and friendship formation. Hence, a major issue in designing more responsive environments is developing strategies that increase "environment-function fit." This concept means that students or groups exercise control in the ecological sense—that is, they are able to engage in activities under conditions that promote a congruence among setting, type of activity, and occasion (Baron, 1979). For example, students are able to exercise control over studying when they are able to study when they want to, under conditions likely to promote effective studying—when they can implement desired levels of privacy and stimulation. When students experience environment-function fit, their environment is manageable; it is relatively predictable and controllable. On the other hand, "non-fitting environments" often restrict freedom, constrain behavior, and in effect produce a sense of helplessness (Sherrod and Cohen, 1978).

Territoriality. The third theory of use to residence educators is territoriality—a primary mechanism that mediates human social behavior and the physical environment, thereby enhancing environment-function fit (Ardrey, 1966; Bakker and Bakker-Rabdau, 1978; Hall, 1966; and Mehrabian, 1976, and Mehrabian and Russell, 1974). Territoriality is a rather complex behavioral system that serves many functions common to both animals and man; regulating density and social interaction, organizing behavior, providing areas for privacy and security, reducing conflict and aggression, and insuring social order and group stability (Altman, 1975). Grant (1974) describes the significance of the relationship between territoriality and student development. He suggests that territoriality is one mechanism that is universal to all cultures, supports the development of human beings in a natural manner, and permits individuals to structure their environment in ways that maintain optimal levels of stimulation, privacy, freedom, and order. With doors, rooms, objects, and markers, individuals can regulate the variety and intensity of stimulation in their environment and thereby establish appropriate privacy levels. This is particularly important for protection from excessive or unwanted stimuli. When an individual's optimal level of stimulation is exceeded, the resulting stress must be reduced to avoid both psychological and physical damage (Wohlwill, 1974).

Two studies deal specifically with territorial behavior in college residence halls. Hansen and Altman (1976) found a positive relationship among personalizing student rooms and retention and group stability. Similar results are noted by Schroeder (1976), who reported a 40 percent increase in retention, an 82 percent decline in damages, and a substantial increase in both occupancy and academic achievement following a three-year room and hallway personalization program. These studies suggest that room decorating may be a long-term predictor of retention rates and that the territorial behavior of marking and personalizing space may significantly contribute to positive student development.

To summarize, we have now identified three broad themes that can provide direction for our design efforts. From our study of social climate, we have learned that student satisfaction and growth is promoted by environments that provide a delicate balance between challenge and support dimensions. Similarly, student development is enhanced when students experience congruence between their personal characteristics and certain environmental conditions. Finally, territoriality is a primary mechanism that mediates student behavior and the physical environment and permits students to render environments more predictable and controllable. Now let's translate these theories into practical applications for designing effective residential environments.

Translating Theory to Practice

The dimensions to which these environmental theories may be applied are the social environment, the physical environment, and the interaction between the two. Let us first suggest ways that the social environment can be designed to promote individual and group compatibility.

Matching Roommates. The smallest group, the dyad, is the basic component in a residence hall group. It is important, therefore, to assign roommates in ways that increase student-environment congruence. One method that has proved effective is matching roommates on the basis of personalized compatibility as measured by the Myers-Briggs Type Indicator (MBTI) (Myers, 1962, Myers, 1976). The MBTI is based on Carl Jung's theory of psychological type. Briefly, the theory states that "much apparent random variation in human behavior is actually quite orderly and consistent, being caused by certain basic differences in mental functioning" (Myers, 1962, p. 51). These basic differences result from the way people prefer to use their various mental processes. Scores obtained from the MBTI indicate a person's preference for the following four dichotomous dimensions: (1) extroversion-introversion (EI)—whether a person prefers to direct the dominant mental process toward the external world of people and things or toward the inner world of concepts and ideas; (2) sensing-intuition (SN)—whether a person prefers to perceive the world in a factual, realistic way or to perceive inherent, imaginative possibilities; (3) thinking-feeling (TF)—whether the individual prefers to arrive at decisions in a logical, orderly fashion or by appreciating personal and interpersonal subjective values; and (4) judging-perceiving (JP)—whether a person prefers to use a judging attitude (thinking or feeling) or a perceptive attitude (sensing or intuition) in dealing with the external world. The SN and TF dimensions are regarded as functions of perception and judgment. Although everyone uses all four functions in varying degrees, each individual tends to prefer one dominant function.

As evidenced by our description of Willard and Sam's relationship, differences in psychological type can cause miscommunication, misunderstanding, and conflict. Obviously, Willard and Sam are opposite types. In Myers-Briggs terminology, Willard is an ESTJ and Sam, an ENFP. Extraversion is the only mental process they have in common. They perceive things differently (sensing versus intuition), formulate decisions from different perspectives (thinking versus feeling), and tend to prefer to live their lives in opposing ways (judging and seeking closure versus perceiving and keeping options open). Since they have few things in common, chances are they will not develop a meaningful relationship. However, had they been matched with individuals with similar mental functions, the probability of a compatible relationship would have increased.

Matching roommates on MBTI functions is quite simple. If residence educators want to eradicate incongruence between roommates, then students should be matched on the basis of compatibility. *Compatible* means identical scores. Examples of compatible matchings are pairing ESTJs with ESTJs, and ENFPs with ENFPs. However, if "optimal incongruence" is desired, then student scores should be complementary. *Complementary* is defined as having a common dominant process and different auxiliary processes. Complementary pairing ensures growth within the relationship. A complementary match would be the pair ENFP and ENTP. Intuition (N), the dominant process for both persons, provides a commonality for the relationship. However, the auxiliary functions of thinking (T) and feeling (F) are different for each. Although both these individuals use the intuitive process for perceiving, they make judgments by means of different processes. Through modeling, each individual would inadvertently help the other develop the corresponding behaviors.

The efficacy of matching roommates on the basis of personality compatibility (MBTI) has been demonstrated by Eigenbrod (1969) and Schroeder (1976). The first year this strategy was implemented at Auburn University, requests for roommate changes declined by over 65 percent. In addition, twenty-four pairs of self-selected roommates were randomly picked and their MBTI scores compared. Twenty-one of the twenty-four pairs had matched themselves in the same manner as that employed by the housing staff. The preceding studies imply that matching students on the basis of compatible or complementary types simply increases the probability of friendship.

Matching Suitemates. In an attempt to create a stronger support system in highrise residence halls housing approximately twenty-five hundred students on the Ohio State University campus, residence educators matched suitemates on the basis of compatible MBTI scores. Each floor of the highrise building contained six suites with sixteen residents per suite. Students matched on MBTI scores perceived their environment as emphasizing a much higher degree of emotional support and involvement than students assigned in the traditional fashion (Kalsbeek, 1980). This strategy may be particularly useful to residence educators working in large, complex universities with highrise buildings.

Assigning Students to Floor Units. Friendship patterns, group cohesion, and perserverance in the residence halls also have been facilitated by assigning students to floor units according to dominant (MBTI) personality functions (Schroeder, Warner, and Malone, 1980). One floor unit, for example, was composed of sensing (S) types, another intuitive (N) types, and so forth. The auxiliary process varied within the groups in order to provide an optimally incongruent environment. A major advantage associated with this strategy is that developmental programs can be fitted more easily to student groups that exhibit unique characteristics. For example, intuitive types benefit from time-management programs while assertiveness workshops are particularly helpful to feeling types.

These strategies for improving social environments have been successful in promoting individual and group compatibility. The physical environment also provides opportunities for putting theory into action. Sommer (1974) states that contemporary residence halls represent "hard architecture"—uniform, impersonal, regularized, and generally impervious to human imprint. In the design of these facilities, the old architectural adage "form follows function" was, for the most part, forgotten. The resulting lack of congruence between the design elements (size of room, location of furniture, and distance to lounges) and the activities to be performed in the spaces (studying, sleeping, socializing) is a major contributor to student dissatisfaction. Although financial realities prohibit major renovations of existing facilities, residence educators can apply their knowledge of environmental theory, and specifically territoriality, to assist students restructure residence hall environments to make them more responsive to student needs. Specific goals include overcoming institutional atmospheres; increasing opportunities for privacy and solitude; reducing damage and vandalism; and promoting group interaction, stability, and identity.

Overcoming Institutional Physical Environments. To overcome the depersonalizing effects of traditional institutional decor, residence educators should actively encourage students to personalize their living areas by painting; wallpapering; paneling; adding plants, posters, and drapes; constructing lofts, bookcases, and other furniture; refinishing doors; plastering ceilings; and replacing fixtures. Room painting might include covering the walls with murals, supergraphics, caricatures, and slogans. Perception of room size, degree of pleasantness, and levels of stimulation can be altered by selecting paints that differ in brightness and saturation. In addition, plants—such as hanging baskets, ferns, and palms—add dimensions of life, pleasantness, color, and texture to rooms. When rooms with drab, lifeless walls and sterile furnishings are personalized, they become places where students want to be. In such environments, students feel influential, unrestricted, secure, and in control.

Students are not the only ones who benefit from room personalization. A campus-wide study to assess program impacts revealed that damages, maintenance costs, and attrition significantly declined following program implementation on all campuses surveyed (Schroeder, 1979). For example, Georgia Southwestern College reported a reduction in damage costs of over 300 percent the first year. At Auburn University, women residents in one medium-sized residence hall were furnished paint by the housing office. They painted their rooms and hallways for approximately twelve hundred dollars, considerably less than the sixty-seven thousand dollars proposed by the university's physical plant. These kinds of results are obviously important to everyone who works with the housing program, including business managers, maintenance personnel, and residence educators. A recent publication by Anchors, Schroeder, and Jackson (1978) is a helpful resource for residence educators interested in implementing personalization programs.

Increasing Opportunities for Privacy and Solitude. When two or more students share a room they seldom find privacy and solitude. In addition, privacy within a double room is often prevented by built-in furniture and inflexible arrangements. In such rigid and confined space, students quite naturally and unavoidably encroach on one another's personal space and territory. The result is often miscommunication and conflict.

Although offering more private rooms is an obvious solution to lack of privacy and solitude, current demands for on-campus housing and certain fiscal restraints make this an unrealistic option. However, residence educators can encourage students to redesign the interiors of their rooms by building partitions and lofts and by creating boundaries through placement of bookcases, plants, and desks. Such arrangements help students eliminate undesirable visual stimulation that can interfere with studying and sleeping. This seems to be particularly important for students like Willard Wilson who are "non-screeners" — individuals who are quite aware of minor, subtle changes in the environment as a result of their inability to "tune things out." Thus, even within double rooms, students can to some extent regulate stimulation load and privacy levels.

The establishment of territorial boundaries not only helps to reduce an individual's perceptions of crowding; it also promotes stable group functioning. If two roommates like Willard and Sam spent time clearly defining their living habits early in their relationship by organizing space and functions within their room, they would be able to better accommodate their natural differences in basic needs.

Reducing Damages and Vandalism. Newman's (1972) study of conflict and crime in an urban, low-cost housing project revealed that the highest frequency of crime was in semi-public areas that did were neither easily personalized nor under the control of residents. Since the areas could not easily be marked and controlled by occupants, Newman termed them "nondefensible" territories. Newman's study has important implications for residence educators. In residence halls, hallways and floor lounges have been designed in ways that make surveillance by residents difficult. These spaces have been painted a uniform color and furnished in a bland institutional way. Visitor access is generally not restricted, so residents' control is, at best, minimal. Secondary territories thus become public. They have an extremely high encroachment potential and an institutional, rather than a group, identity. When damages occur in these areas, students rarely exhibit much concern or discomfort primarily because they perceive these public territories as owned and controlled by the institution and not by the house or student group.

If secondary territories such as hallways and lounges are to function as intended, they must be perceived as owned and controlled by the group. To accomplish this, residence educators should encourage students to paint, decorate, or otherwise visibly mark these areas to render them as distinguishable as possible. Such territorial markers will serve a common purpose, "to inform that one is passing from a space which is public, where one's presence is not questioned, through a barrier to a space where one's presence requires justification" (Newman, 1972, p. 63). When a secondary territory such as a hallway is adequately marked and becomes the *common property* of a group, attitudes in the group change. Residents begin to take care of the space and share concern for maintaining it. Students will use these areas in proportion to the amount of time they spend marking and decorating them, and damages will be inversely related to the degree of personalization. Obviously, student motivation to maintain this space will be similarly related to the degree of control they possess in relation to the space. Encroachment by undesirables will also be minimized since the areas have been visually transformed into identifiable group, or defensible, space.

Enhancing Group Interaction, Stability and Identity. By creating effective social climates and encouraging students to personalize primary and secondary space, residence educators can begin to foster a sense of community. Community is sustained when residential facilities encourage frequent interaction among students. However, as previously indicated, most group socializing areas are remote and inaccessible from areas central to the daily lives of students. As a result, students like Sam Hudson use their corridor bedrooms as entertaining and socializing space. Naturally, such an arrangement might interfere with Sam's roommate's needs to engage in activities that require a relative degree of privacy. To overcome these problems, residence educators could convert into group rooms student rooms centrally located along corridors. Residents could then design, personalize, and control these areas according to their own needs and desires. This strategy has already been implemented at Auburn University, and research obtained from a longitudinal study indicated that freshman males who lived on floor units with group rooms manifested more concern for others, emphasized more open and honest communication, engaged in more pleasant social interaction, and placed a greater emphasis on academic accomplishments and other scholarly activities than freshmen on traditional halls without group rooms (West, Warner, and Schroeder, 1979).

Besides primary and secondary spaces, students also need large areas where active, stimulating behavior can take place. After students have been studying for a while, they often need a break to listen to records, talk to neighbors, or engage in physical activity. Naturally, these activities may disrupt other students sleeping or studying nearby and may take a toll on physical facilities. This situation can be avoided if residence educators create stimulation zones where exciting activities are expected and encouraged. Converting a large public lounge into a comprehensive health club with a variety of exercise equipment (Schroeder and Connors, 1977) or a recreation area with pinball machines, table games, loud music, and exciting colors gives students a variety of novel, intense, and complex stimuli. Such redesign efforts enhance social interaction and provide for privacy, security, and the reduction of conflicts in primary and secondary territories (Jackson and Schroeder, 1976).

Conclusion

Although the proposition that environments exert powerful effects on human behavior is widely accepted, in many residence halls it is the individual students, and not the environment, who remain the primary target for change. All too often students are expected to adjust and accommodate themselves to prevailing physical and social environments, and they are rarely provided opportunities to change or redesign these environments to make them more responsive to their own needs and personal growth goals. As a result, students may pay a high adaptation cost in terms of dissatisfaction, marginal performance, instability, and avoidance of the environment. Residence educators have traditionally reacted to these concerns by using corrective and remedial strategies to increase coping skills in students rather than targeting staff efforts at reducing or eliminating the negative or self-defeating milieu dimensions. Rigid adherence to these approaches appears to imply this viewpoint: "If the shoe doesn't fit, there must be something wrong with your foot."

Although our traditional approach to residence education has increased the quality of life for many students, it represents a rather narrow, one-sided approach. By adopting an environmental perspective—a perspective that focuses on the transactions between students and their physical environments—residence educators can create a balanced and complete approach to facilitating student development in residence halls.

References

Altman, I. *The Environment and Social Behavior.* Monterey, Calif.: Brooks/Cole, 1975.

Anchors, S., Schroeder, C., and Jackson, S. *Making Yourself at Home: A Practical Guide to Restructuring and Personalizing Your Residence Hall Environment.* Cincinnati, Ohio: American College Personnel Association, 1978.

Ardrey, R. *The Territorial Imperative.* New York: Atheneum, 1966.

Bakker, C. and Bakker-Rabdau, M. *No Trespassing: Explorations in Human Territoriality.* San Francisco: Chandler, 1978.

Baron, R. "Ecological Approaches to Understanding Human Crowding." *Journal of Population,* 1979, *2,* 235–258.

Baron, R., Mandel, D., Adams, C., and Griffen, L. "Effects of Social Density in University Residential Environments." *Journal of Personality and Social Psychology,* 1976, *34,* 434–446.

Baum, A., Aiello, J., and Colesnick, L. "Crowding and Personal Control: Social Density and the Development of Learned Helplessness." *Journal of Personality and Social Psychology,* 1978, *36,* 1000–1011.

Brown, R. "Manipulation of the Environmental Press in a College Residence Hall." *Personnel and Guidance Journal,* 1968, *46,* 555–560.

Eigenbrod, F. "The Effects of Territory and Personality Compatibility on Identity and Security." Unpublished doctoral dissertation, Department of Administration and Higher Education, Michigan State University, 1969.

Feldman, K., and Newcomb, T. *The Impact of College on Students.* San Francisco: Jossey-Bass, 1969.

Gerst, M., and Sweetwood, H. "Correlates of Dormitory Social Climate." *Environment and Behavior,* 1973, *5,* 440–463.

Grant, H. W. "Humanizing the Residence Hall Environment." In D. DeCoster and P. Mable (Eds.), *Student Development and Education in College Residence Halls.* Cincinnati, Ohio: American College Personnel Association, 1974.

Hall, E. *The Hidden Dimension.* New York: Doubleday, 1966.

Hansen, W., and Altman, I. "Decorating Personal Places: A Descriptive Analysis." *Environment and Behavior,* 1976, *8,* 491–504.

Heilweil, M. "The Influence of Dormitory Architecture on Resident Behavior." *Environment and Behavior,* 1973, *5,* 377–411.

High, T., and Sundstrom, E. "Room Flexibility and Space Use in a Dormitory." *Environment and Behavior,* 1977, *9,* 81–90.

Holahan, C., and Wilcox, B. "Residential Satisfaction and Friendship Formation in High and Low-Rise Student Housing: An Interactional Analysis." *Journal of Educational Psychology,* 1978, *70,* 237–241.

Holland, J. *Making Vocational Choices: A Theory of Careers.* Englewood Cliffs, N.J.: Prentice-Hall, 1973.

Jackson, G., and Schroeder, C. "Behavioral Zoning for Stimulation Seekers." *Journal of College and University Student Housing,* 1976, *6,* 16–20.

Kalsbeek, D. "Balancing the Support-Challenge Ratio in Residence Hall Environments: A Study of the Effects of Roommate Matching by Personality Type Compared to Standard Procedures on Student Perceptions of Social Climate." Unpublished master's thesis, Department of Education, Ohio State University, 1980.

Mehrabian, A. *Public Places and Private Spaces.* New York: Basic Books, 1976.

Mehrabian, A., and Russell, J. *An Approach to Environmental Psychology.* Cambridge, Mass.: M.I.T. Press, 1974.

Montgomery, J., McLaughlin, G., Fawcett, L., Pedigo, E., and Ward, S. "The Impact of Different Residence Hall Environments on Student Attitudes." *Journal of College Student Personnel,* 1975, *16,* 389–393.

Myers, I. *Myers-Briggs Type Indicator: Manual.* Princeton, N.J.: Educational Testing Service, 1962.

Myers, I. *Introduction to Type.* Gainesville, Fla.: Center for the Applications of Psychological Type, 1976.

Newman, O. *Defensible Space.* New York: Macmillan, 1972.

Sanford, N. *Where Colleges Fail.* San Francisco: Jossey-Bass, 1967.

Schroeder, C. "New Strategies for Structuring Residential Environments." *Journal of College Student Personnel,* 1976, *17,* 386–390.

Schroeder, C. "Territoriality: Conceptual and Methodological Issues for Residence Educators." *Journal of College and University Student Housing,* 1979, *8,* 9–15.

Schroeder, C., and Belmonte, A. "The Influence of Residential Environment on Prepharmacy Student Achievement and Satisfaction." *American Journal of Pharmaceutical Education,* 1979, *43,* 16–19.

Schroeder, C., and Connors, M. "A Physical Development Program for College Students." *Journal of College Student Personnel,* 1977, *18,* 523.

Schroeder, C., Warner, R., and Malone, D. "Effects of Assignment to Living Units by Personality Types on Environmental Perceptions and Student Development." *Journal of College Student Personnel,* 1980, in press.

Sherrod, D., and Cohen, S. "Density, Personal Control, and Design." In S. Kaplan and R. Kaplan (Eds.), *Humanscape: Environments for People.* North Scituate, Mass.: Duxbury Press, 1978.

Sommer, R. *Tight Spaces: Hard Architecture and How to Humanize It.* Englewood Cliffs, N.J.: Prentice-Hall, 1974.

Titus, C. "Housing for Today's Student." *Journal of College and University Student Housing,* 1973, *3,* 4–7.

Valines, S., and Baum, A. "Residential Group Size, Social Interaction, and Crowding." *Environment and Behavior,* 1973, *5,* 421–439.

West, N., Warner, R., and Schroeder, C. "The Group Room: An Aid to Student Development." *Journal of College and University Student Housing,* 1979, *9,* 20–24.

Wohlwill, J. "Human Adaptation to Levels of Environmental Stimulation." *Human Ecology,* 1974, *2,* 127–147.

Charles C. Schroeder is dean of students and assistant professor of psychology at Mercer University, Macon, Georgia. He has made many contributions to professional journals and books. Schroeder is the former chairperson of Commission III (Residence Halls) of the American College Personnel Association, and a frequent presenter at regional and national conferences.

Although most student affairs administrators agree that living
learning programs integrate social and intellectual development,
it is not always clear how to create such an environment.
This chapter provides a practical model for structuring
residence halls as living learning centers.

Environmental Structuring: Residence Halls as Living Learning Centers

Linda Pedretty Rowe

The purposes of this chapter are twofold. One general purpose is to identify the philosophical basis for the development of living learning centers, to describe various living learning center structures, and to develop an operational definition of living learning centers. The second general purpose is to examine ten components of the living learning center and explore areas of concern within each of the ten components.

Philosophical Bases

On most residential college and university campuses one can expect to find student affairs administrators agreeing on this concept: students should live in an environment that offers them more than simply a place to eat and sleep. Thus the role of the residence life personnel or "residence educators" is that of structuring the residential environment.

The living learning residential model arose largely from a desire on the part of students and educators to reaffirm the relevance of education to daily life and vice versa—a theme which harks back to the Oxford and Cambridge residential colleges in which students and faculty lived, ate, and studied together. Recapturing a sense of intellectual intimacy has particularly strong appeal on larger campuses where the mission of educating the whole person is often lost beneath the burdens of size and cost-effectiveness.

The philosophical bases for the living learning center (LLC) model are as old as the Oxford model and as new as recent student personnel literature. Riker (1965) envisions college housing as learning centers and maintains that one of the roles of the residence educator should be to help students integrate their collegiate experiences (1974). Brown (1974) suggests that residence education become a form of "social engineering" and briefly discusses five ways in which college housing could systhesize academic and extracurricular activities: having faculty discussions in the halls, teaching regular classes within housing units, establishing living learning environments, establishing coed halls, and merging academic and student development. DeCoster and Mable (1974) stress that "social and environmental realities" must be recognized. They see residence educators as catalysts, consultants, and resources in uniting educational and social opportunities with student leisure time.

Living Learning Center Structures

Endeavors to facilitate the growth of the student as a total person have included a striking variety of special life-style options for campus residents. Although most student development practitioners agree that these programs aim to combine social and intellectual development, it is not always clear exactly how to combine the two or in what settings. Cooperative or communal living arrangements, intentional democratic communities, honors housing, thematic units, residential colleges, language houses, and living learning centers are just a few examples of attempts to integrate aspects of the student's learning milieu within his or her place of residence.

Rising interest in the living learning center as a special type of residential community for students has led to numerous experiments in living learning across the country. The application of the term *LLC* to academic-residential (and some nonresidential) units is widespread; it is apparently used to designate a wide range of educational and environmental structures.

The varied types of programs that are known as living learning centers can be envisioned on a continuum, proceeding from the least structured to the most structured as follows:

Special Interest Units. Usually a hall, corridor, or set of suites designated for students who share an interest, these units emphasize programming related to a theme and the exploration of special interests through affiliation with others during extracurricular hours. Topics range from astronomy to crafts to political activism. A faculty associate or staff member(s) specially selected for expertise on the theme may be involved with the unit.

Like-Major Units. Somewhat more formal than special interest housing, these programs are intended for students of same or similar majors. Emphasis is placed on study groups, the availability of major-related resources within the residence (computer terminals, art studios, or specialized libraries, for example), and the enhancement of learning through sharing. Programming is related to the students' field of study. A faculty adviser generally works with the unit. Honors housing and foreign language residence halls are classified with the special interest and like-major options.

Units with Noncredit Classes and Programming. These units offer structured noncredit experiences to residents. Generally, the student makes a commitment to participate in the planned activities — a more formal relationship to the unit than that expected in special interest and like-major units. Experiences may center on a particular theme, such as music, in which students set aside a certain amount of time for ensemble playing; or the program may be directed to specific goals, such as achieving personal growth or developing leadership skills. Appropriate resource personnel maintain a close relationship (perhaps by living in) with the unit.

Units Offering Regularly Scheduled Classes. Sections of popular courses or discussion classes meet in classroom space within the residence center. Class enrollment in this type of program is generally limited to center residents. Faculty office space may be located in the center. Emphasis is placed on close involvement with faculty members; on small, more intimate classroom experiences; and on merging the academic with the social milieu.

Units with Unique or Experimental Programs. In an effort to provide personalized learning experiences, these residences offer special credit classes, designed by students and/or faculty, that allow students to pursue unique, experimental subject matter. For example, students may be granted academic credit for community volunteer projects or for dramatic productions which they write and stage. Students almost always must make a commitment to participate in the program. Most of these units function at least partially under the direction of a faculty member or academic department.

Residential Colleges. Closest to the Oxford residential model, these mini-colleges generally function as degree-granting entities. Students living together pursue all or a significant portion of their academic careers within the residential college too. This most structured of the living learning options has an academic staff or faculty, dean(s), or tutors. Ideally, faculty members live within the college itself.

Glancing over this continuum of residential options, it becomes clear that the first two types of programs, interest units and like-major units, differ significantly in their degree of structure from the last type, residential colleges. Distinctions between existing residential education options may not be as precise as they appear here. Nevertheless, while each of these options is certainly a living learning program in the sense that it fosters some kind of experiential education or facilitates the integration of academics into residence life, to call all of them living learning centers is to court confusion. The LLC should be recognized as a specific type of college housing program, no more or less valid than any other, but clearly identifiable and describable.

A Living Learning Center Definition

In March 1977, under the auspices of Commission III, "Student Residence Programs," of the American College Personnel Association, a task force on living learning centers was established. It expressly sought "to clarify the meaning of 'living learning center' for the student personnel profession, specifically for residence educators, and to develop a model of the LLC as a collaborative venture into student development" (Rowe and others, 1979, p. 6).

The LLC definition conceived by the task force had to be precise enough to give shape to the LLC concept yet broad enough to allow for adaptation in diverse campus settings. The task force mandated that the definition reflect the current state of the art in LLCs throughout the country.

Materials and comments were collected from LLC administrators and student development theorists. By 1979, the task force had constructed a theoretical model of the LLC based on student development philosophy and thorough observation of and experience with living learning programs. The following definition is at the same time philosophically idealistic and reflective of actual living learning practice:

> *A Living Learning Center* is a residence unit which seeks to integrate the student's academic experience with his or her living environment. The goals of affective, cognitive, and physical growth and development of the resident are pursued through intentional provision of formal and/or informal . . . learning experiences. The LLC is not a degree-granting entity. Student residence in the LLC is voluntary, contingent upon some form of application/selection process. Academic support as well as student affairs support is provided for the LLC and may include facilities, services, ongoing faculty participation, and/or a programming budget (Rowe and others, 1979, p. 21).

Within this framework the LLC is seen to embody the characteristics of the third, fourth, and fifth programs listed in the continuum above. That is, it offers noncredit classes and programming, offers regularly scheduled classes and is—on its campus—a unique or experimental program. Some kind of academic accountability or validity is lent to the LLC's educational programming at all levels.

This recognition of the student's living learning experiences can be viewed from two different perspectives: either informal learning experiences can be given academic structure or academic matters can be brought into the arena of experience. In the first, the student's personal development within the community becomes the topic of study in a course or project. A course offered at the University of Florida entitled "Freshman Leadership" is an example. This course gives academic credit to supervised groups of freshmen who meet in residence halls to explore group dynamics and leadership techniques relevant to their growth as members of the community. Informal, experiential learnings are drawn into the academic arena, giving affective learnings cognitive validity. In the second instance, traditional academic courses are integrated into the less formal milieu of the living unit. Residents of the University of Michigan's Pilot Program are required to participate in a one-credit "Theme Experience" aimed at drawing students together to explore a predesignated broad intellectual issue and to examine its relevance to their lives. Thus academic learning is pulled into the living environment.

The LLC is both an experimental forum for students — students are given the support and opportunities to explore new learnings and activities that meet their needs — and an experimental forum of ideas — faculty members are given the support and the opportunities to explore new teaching methods, new ideas, and new roles which express academic values.

This double focus is common to LLCs. The University of Vermont's LLC brochure, for instance, states that the center strives to promote academic exchange among academic departments and foster research into the ways students learn. The Vermont program wants students to take initiative and responsibility for their own education and seeks to integrate the social and academic aspects of students' lives. Indiana University's LLC and Michigan's Pilot Program also articulate both dedication to meeting student needs and commitment to educational experimentation. Student needs and faculty needs marry in a common forum of learning in which all vested interests participate: students are attracted to the LLC because it is a place where they can "do their own thing"; academicians are attracted to the LLC because it offers a setting for intellectual activism.

Components of the Living Learning Center

The LLC model can be divided into ten components. These aspects of the model should be examined carefully by residence educators, for they suggest the lines along which LLCs can develop.

Philosophy and Goals. The identification of goals is an important first step in building the LLC. LLCs should have an articulated philosophy and clearly stated goals that participants can reasonably expect to achieve. The following goals appear frequently in mission statements collected from a dozen LLCs:

- To provide opportunities for students to pursue an academic lifestyle
- To encourage interdisciplinary study
- To foster peer support for learning
- To allow students input in and control over curriculum and programs
- To encourage close student-faculty relationships
- To bridge the gap between cognitive and affective development

The purpose of Unit One as stated in University of Illinois brochures is fairly typical. Flexibility is stressed; Unit One objectives develop and change with the changing priorities, skills, and interest of students and staff. An unchanging objective, however, is to encourage students to use university resources to achieve personal and educational objectives.

Yet if goals are too general and vague, the LLC may begin to flounder and drift, without direction. Chamberlain (1979) concludes that a lack of specificity of purpose compromised the "uniqueness" as an institution of Indiana University's LLC, although this vagueness was not a serious concern to those directly in the program. To some extent, LLCs must be ready to alter their goals and direction as clientele needs and interests change. Faculty, students, and staff should meet regularly to refresh their objectives and keep the program on track.

Administration. Miller and Prince (1976) assert that student development must be the shared responsibility of all campus groups—faculty, staff, and students. Just as the LLC must integrate learnings, so too must it aspire to involve diverse constituencies in facilitating student development. Under optimum conditions, this collaboration assures that every area of campus expertise will be pooled in support of the student. If an LLC is to live up to the terms of its definition it must be founded in cooperation among all campus sectors. This means financial and ideological support on the part of student affairs, academic departments, student government, and facilities management personnel, all of whom participate equally and enthusiastically. Each group must commit itself to openness and innovation, and perhaps be willing to agree that another perspective is as valid as its own. Even if faculty and students understand student development theory, they will not necessarily respect it. Similarly, residence educators involved with LLCs are sometimes surprisingly reluctant to admit that traditional academic methods—lectures, debates, term papers—can be as meaningful to the student as the more informal, interactive strategies of their profession.

From a practical standpoint achieving cooperation may prove difficult. Brown (1978, p. 11) asks, "How is the often-used expression *collaboration* to be brought into reality?" He notes that the "success of the [student development] model is highly dependent upon the particular people fitting various roles, which it should be to some extent, but not entirely" (p. 11). Continuing dialogue, shared administrative responsibilities, and frequent face-to-face contacts foster a climate of trust and mutual understanding among LLC collaborators. Student development administrators should use whatever skills they possess to facilitate productive interaction in the LLC. Structures that promote collaboration include faculty/staff advisory boards, student/faculty curriculum planning and design committees, faculty members-in-residence, and shared administrative roles for academic personnel and residence educators.

Faculty involvement and support are vitally important elements of the LLC. The presence in the center of an academic administrator enhances the academic validity of the program, as does LLC accountability to one or more academic departments. Most LLC staffs include faculty members as directors, instructors, advisers, tutors, or consultants. Indeed, some LLCs are faculty-generated projects—Illinois' Unit One, for example.

For the LLC program initiated by student affairs professionals, however, gaining faculty support may be very difficult. For instance, the designers of the Shaw Hall Living Learning program at Syracuse University discovered that it was relatively easy to obtain verbal support from academic departments, but that getting financial or resource assistance required much more persuasion. Residence educators must be prepared to "sell" the LLC to the academic departments, identifying and emphasizing those elements of the program that will be most attractive to professors.

They might begin by hosting university courses within the residence center and inviting faculty advisers and liaisons (lured by free meals in dining halls or by office space) to participate in the LLC. Experience at the Indiana University LLC reveals that faculty members find invitations to participate especially appealing when they are issued by students. Professors also often appreciate opportunities to affiliate with other faculty members—particularly those outside their own disciplines—in the living learning setting.

Cultivating strong relationships between the LLC and just one or two faculty supporters is a highly recommended strategy, especially in the initial stages of the program. The identification and involvement of a key academic person—someone with top credentials and influence who holds the respect of his or her colleagues—can be the single most significant factor in ensuring continuing faculty support for the program.

Although faculty support is essential, student involvement in the design, administration, and implementation of the LLC program underlies the center's success as a learning community. LLC administrators must ensure that opportunities for student involvement exist at every step of program development.

Vermont's LLC offers a procedure for students to design educational programs; at Illinois' Unit One, student committees chart the course of center programming; and at Indiana's LLC one of the elected student government positions is academic vice-president. This vice-president chairs the curriculum committee, serves on the faculty-staff advisory board, and promotes educational activities in the center. That students should participate actively in directing their programs is a point vehemently and repeatedly stressed in virtually all the literature published by living learning centers.

Selections, Contracts, and Requirements. A characteristic of the LLC is some type of application/selection process for students. The general rule seems to be self-selection: if the student is attracted by the program and willing to take the time to submit an application, then he or she is deemed sufficiently committed to the center to participate.

Objective criteria such as grade point average or academic prerequisites may be considered in programs where sophisticated experimental credit courses are offered. Project PLUS at The College of William and Mary and Vermont's LLC are examples. Usually, LLCs look for the more intangible qualities of motivation, curiosity, and community commitment. Indiana University screens its applications for membership and asks those students who seem overly casual in their interest to reapply. Syracuse's Shaw Hall opens its doors initially to all interested comers, but reserves the right to interview returning students when their commitment to the program is in question.

Although there appears to be no rule regarding the class of LLC participants, the LLC has traditionally been envisioned as a freshman and sophomore venture. Perhaps this is because during the first two years the student has not yet settled into a major and has the flexibility to explore various learning opportunities. While many LLCs allow residents to remain members of the community throughout their academic careers, the more academically structured programs (William and Mary's Project PLUS, Ball State's Carmichael Project) limit involvement to specific undergraduate years.

In addition to establishing a systematic procedure for assigning students to the LLC, the LLC must present students with a fairly clear set of expectations for participation. A minimal participation level that is consistent with the center's philosophy should be required of students. Vermont's LLC, Michigan's Pilot Program, and Syracuse's Shaw Hall ask students to enter into a contract or agreement that solidifies their commitment to the program. Continuing in the program may be contingent upon successful commitment to the contract.

Size and Characteristics of the Resident Population. The LLCs reviewed here range in size from thirty-five (Northwestern's College of Community Studies) to eight hundred (Ball State's Carmichael Residential Instruction Program) residents. Some LLC programs in California institutions cross residence hall lines and theoretically include more students than Ball State's. More than half of single hall LLCs have over three hundred students.

By virtue of their shared commitment to the LLC's philosophy and participation in common activities, LLC residents gain a sense of belonging and community. In view of the LLC's emphasis on community participation, the size of the program should not be too great to prohibit face-to-face interaction and a sense of closeness among students. Yet it would be surprising to find a person whose circle of friends and acquaintances exceeds two hundred individuals. Except in the smallest programs (twenty-five to fifty students), the residence educators is unrealistic to expect all residents to work and socialize as a single group.

Identification with subgroups is inevitable and may lead to cliques and thus student frustration if alternatives are not encouraged. Larger LLCs should provide opportunities for students to identify with subcommunities — interest corridors, study groups, committees, clubs, and the like. Expansion as a symbol of success is not necessarily to be valued by the LLC; most of those programs studied impose an upper limit on enrollments.

Ideally, the LLC is self-contained. It has exclusive use of its residential facilities. The presence of nonprogram students can be problematic. They may feel alienated and isolated because they do not share the other residents' commitment to the LLC. Magnarella (1979) found that nonprogram students' perceptions of the Vermont LLC were most positive when they were housed together rather than dispersed among program participants.

LLC student populations generally prove to be homogeneous in outlook and background though not in academic majors (Magnarella, 1975), factors likely to be beneficial to their sense of community (DeCoster and Mable, 1974). Chamberlain (1979, p. 247) observes that while Indiana University's LLC residents are comparable to students in other halls with regard to grade point average and choice of academic major, they tend "to be more psychologically independent, creative, and liberal in . . . outlook" than their peers. It has not been shown that these differences are attributable to the LLC experience. Rather, it appears that they are personality factors that influence the decision to live in the LLC.

LLCs do not usually consider choice of academic major when they screen students. However, a number of the LLCs studied (Illinois' Unit One, Indiana's LLC, William and Mary's Project PLUS, and Michigan's Pilot Program, for example) require a commitment to liberal arts or to interdisciplinary education. LLCs thus attract intellectually enthusiastic, motivated, creative undergraduates whose home and secondary school backgrounds have prepared them for college life.

Programming. The cocurricular programs at the LLC should reflect the character of its academic experiences and remain consistent with the center's educational and developmental goals. Faculty lectures, round-table discussions, language tables in the dining hall, crafts instruction, theater groups, field trips, and human growth workshops begin a long list of appropriate activities.

Generally, a portion of the LLC budget is earmarked for special cultural opportunities. At Unit One (University of Illinois), an artist-in-residence program, which brings ten creative people to the center each year, is funded by the College of Liberal Arts and Sciences and the Housing Division. The Carmichael Program (Ball State University) sponsors a repertory theater group and, Indiana University's LLC funds a magazine of student poetry.

Student governments should be encouraged to keep the LLC's mission in mind when designing social and recreational activities. Receptions for campus visitors, group trips to plays and concerts, and "college bowl" quiz contests are among the options available. In addition, LLCs should seize every opportunity to use free campus and community programs. These include faculty lectures, films from local libraries, mini-courses and demonstrations—a whole range of resources waiting to be tapped. By no means should attendance be limited to LLC participants. By offering its space and its personnel for programs of campus-wide interest, the LLC can perform a valuable outreach function and establish an attractive connection between itself and other segments of the campus community.

Relationship to the University at Large. The LLC has a responsibility not only to meet student needs but also to serve as a forum for experimental inquiry and innovation in instruction. For instance, the LLC may be able to offer a faculty member an opportunity to engage in a pet research project with a small group of motivated undergraduates. The experimental course series at

Vermont's and Indiana's LLCs are envisioned as opportunities for professors to try out and develop new courses for eventual inclusion in the university-wide curriculum.

The LLC administrator strives constantly to keep other university personnel aware of the center's activities. If other departments are asked to contribute funds or resources to the LLC, then they should understand what the LLC contributes to them.

Budget and Funding. Funding is a concern of every program director today since the LLC is likely to be in the unstable position characteristic of any special program. Residence educators can make good use of the collaborative model in funding the LLC because it is usually easier to take a little money from several budgets than a lot from one. The various funding models employed by LLCs include:

1. *Designated LLC Funds*—Monies from academic and/or student affairs budgets are turned over to LLC administrators to disburse. Expenses may include salaries, equipment, programming, facilities, or honoraria.

2. *Departmental Sponsorship*—In this plan one or more departments earmark portions of their budgets to defray, for example, the cost of faculty telephone lines for the LLC, resident assistant salaries, or duplicating materials. In this model the funding departments usually demand some control over the activities of the LLC.

3. *Departmental Support*—This plan does not involve direct funding, but the willingness of various departments to contribute their resources to the LLC. Departments can support by releasing faculty to teach at the LLC, lending equipment such as videotape machines or automobiles, and donating office supplies.

4. *Student Fees*—Fees can be collected separately or as part of student rent and are used for center activities. Special care must be taken to insure that students have at least a partial say in determining how the money is spent.

No model need exclude another. Indeed, most LLCs adopt an eclectic approach: they get whatever they can from wherever they can. Funds from usual sources may be supplemented with special donations and grants. Some LLC programs, such as artist-in-residence series or experimental curriculum designs, lend themselves to federal or private grant proposals.

Staff and Staff Training. A few models for faculty staffing have been mentioned. Professors and instructors may be employed directly by the center or may serve in associate capacities. LLC faculty members are most often supervised by an academic dean or similar figure, who may or may not be the chief LLC administrator.

In the ideal model, faculty, staff, and students share in the administration of the LLC. The center becomes an integrated program, not merely a collection of separate operations housed in one building. This model carries significant implications for student personnel administrators who are charged with ensuring that the residential staff reflects the philosophy of the LLC.

At Indiana University's LLC, for example, the "Resident Fellows" (undergraduate and graduate paraprofessional staff members) are selected for their commitment to intellectual inquiry, for their ability to serve as positive academic role models, and for the other qualifications expected in resident assistants. The University of Nebraska's Centennial Educational Program requires its student assistants to have spent some time as program members. In contrast, the director of Unit One (University of Illinois) reported that, before he corrected the problem, his program experienced difficulties because the housing office assigned the unit's resident assistant staff with no particular consideration for the goals of the LLC. The staff was not always sensitive to the program's needs and thus did not support a living learning environment at its fundamental level—the students' living space.

Essential features of any LLC's staff training plan should be an emphasis on understanding the LLC's goals and philosophy and developing strategies for integrating the cognitive and affective experiences of the students.

Facilities. The facilities available in the LLC's physical plant should reflect the integration of learnings that the LLC attempts. That is, LLCs should offer space for faculty offices, for cultural expression, for socialization, and for study. This space should be somewhat flexible, allowing students to personalize their environment. Adequately equipped, quiet classroom space is mandatory. Departments have been known to withdraw their classes from residence halls because professors complained of excessive outside noise, insufficient seating, or lack of blackboards and chalk. Appointments that generate a warm atmosphere foster community and individual growth. DeCoster and Mable (1974) observe that adequate physical facilities are an essential component of a successful residence program. Students will be less likely to perceive their LLC as an intellectually stimulating environment if, for instance, the halls are noisy or the showers don't work.

The LLC at the University of Vermont was designed specifically to serve as a living learning center. This LLC is a complex of six interconnected buildings that house suites for students, apartments for faculty and visiting scholars, instructional classrooms, recreational rooms, a dining area, a snack bar, and common lounges and meeting rooms. Students live in suites of five to seven persons. Suitemates are brought together by common interests.

Magnarella (1975, p. 304) found that this design acts in some respects as "a limiting or boundary-maintaining factor" and causes students to "complain that their acquaintanceships rarely extend beyond their entry or building wing." Nevertheless, when asked what aspect of the LLC they liked best, the students most frequently replied, "LLC facilities" (Magnarella, 1979, p. 6).

Indiana University's LLC, in contrast to the Vermont LLC, is located in pre–World War II collegiate-tutor dormitory buildings adapted for use as a living learning center. Here again, it appears that the uniqueness of the physical facilities are of major importance in attracting program participants. Chamberlain (1979, p. 252) went so far as to suggest "that without the physical facility the . . . LLC would probably be without a significant part of its raison d'être."

Evaluation. It is essential that the LLC continually evaluate its process and its appeal. Criteria for evaluation may be imposed by the institution at large, which is usually interested in assessing the LLC's contribution to campus life and institutional missions. Or evaluation criteria may be internally generated and be designed to assess student satisfaction and achievement within the program. Some difficulty exists in trying to evaluate the LLC on a purely objective basis. How does one quantify the enrichment of student life or the integration of cognitive and affective development?

Williams and Reilley (1974) give a fine overview of the research on the impact of LLCs on students. The authors conclude that no clear confirmation exists in support of the claim that LLCs provide a more "intellectual environment" than other halls or that they offer "an advantage in terms of student-faculty relationships" (p. 227). Student satisfaction with LLCs appears to be high, however.

Any number of evaluative models will help in assessing student opinion of the LLC. Centra (1968) administered a modified form of the College and University Environment Scales Questionnaire to undergraduates randomly selected from living learning halls and conventional halls at a large university and compared student perceptions of their living environments. Magnarella (1975, 1979), an anthropologist, viewed the LLC from the perspective of his discipline and used questionnaires, interviews, and first-hand observation, again for the purpose of comparing LLC and non-LLC student perceptions of their environments.

The ecosystem approach (Schuh, 1979) allows the residence educator to survey clientele satisfaction of only those program elements that can be changed. Problem areas are readily identified and prioritized through this model. The academic institution-building model (Chamberlain, 1979), on the other hand, views the LLC from the outside, assessing its achievement and uniqueness as a program in relation to other university programs — a measure useful when the objective is to determine the LLC's role in the context of its environment.

Additional research — particularly longitudinal studies — is required to assess the LLC's impact on its students and to identify those individuals most benefited by it.

Summary

The living learning center model of environmental structuring offers residence educators a format for promoting the growth and education of the student as a whole person. Yet, like any model, it is far more challenging to implement than to describe. Practical experience indicates that survival of a living learning program is connected to paying careful attention to the ten elements of the model discussed above. Strong academic support, adequate facilities, a reasonably small population, student involvement in administration, and an openness to modification ensure the viability of the LLC.

Seen as a focal point for student development, the LLC offers opportunities for cognitive growth and development through classes and discussion groups; opportunities for affective growth and development through social functions, coeducational living, and developmental programming; and opportunities for physical well-being through appropriate programming and recreational facilities. Ideally, LLC residents grow and experiment within their living environment to achieve the integration of ideas and feelings that is the key to education.

Student personnel administrators are cautioned, however, against becoming too enamored with this ideal. LLCs may mistakenly attempt to be all things to all students, forgetting that the students' milieu encompasses the campus and community. The LLC is an enriched residence program and an integral part of the broader college or university experience. It is not a panacea. Student needs and learning styles vary and so should campus residence options. The challenge to those responsible for the development of living learning centers is to tailor the program to meet the needs of students within an acceptable framework that will satisfy institutional concerns. Since so many successful living learning centers have been established, it is clear that the most important ingredient in the establishment of the living learning center is the institution's will to do so. Given that resolution, the balance of the process will follow naturally. However, without a strong institutional commitment to the living learning centers, establishing one will be fraught with problems and ultimately doomed to failure.

References

Brown, R. D. "Student Development and Residence Education: Should It Be Social Engineering?" In D. DeCoster and P. Mable (Eds.), *Student Development and Education in College Residence Halls.* Cincinnati, Ohio: American College Personnel Association, 1974.

Brown, R. D. "The Dialogue Should Continue." *ACPA Developments,* Spring 1978, p. 11.

Centra, J. A. "Student Perceptions of Residence Hall Environments: Living Learning vs. Conventional Units." *Journal of College Student Personnel,* 1968, *4,* 266–272.

Chamberlain, P. C. "Evaluating a Living-Learning Program." In G. Kuh (Ed.), *Evaluation in Student Affairs.* Cincinnati, Ohio: American College Personnel Association, 1979.

DeCoster, D. A., and Mable, P. "Residence Education: Purpose and Process." In D. DeCoster and P. Mable (Eds.), *Student Development and Education in College Residence Halls.* Cincinnati, Ohio: American College Personnel Association, 1974.

Magnarella, P. J. "The University of Vermont's Living Learning Center: A First-Year Appraisal." *Journal of College Student Personnel,* 1975, *4,* 300–305.

Magnarella, P. J. "The Continuing Evaluation of a Living Learning Center." *Journal of College Student Personnel,* 1979, *20*(1), 4–9.

Miller, T. K., and Prince, J. S. *The Future of Student Affairs: A Guide to Student Development for Tomorrow's Higher Education.* San Francisco: Jossey-Bass, 1976.

Riker, H. C. *College Housing as Learning Centers.* Cincinnati, Ohio: American College Personnel Association, 1965.

Riker, H. C. "The Role of Residence Educators." In D. DeCoster and P. Mable (Eds.), *Student Development and Education in College Residence Halls.* Cincinnati, Ohio: American College Personnel Association, 1974.

Rowe, L. P., and others. "Living Learning Centers: A Philosophical and Resource Guide for Residence Educators." Bloomington, Ind.: Commission III, American College Personnel Association, 1979.

Schuh, J. H. "Assessment and Redesign in Residence Halls." *New Directions for Student Services: Redesigning Campus Environments,* no. 8. San Francisco: Jossey-Bass, 1979.

Williams, D. E., and Reilley, R. R. "The Impact of Residence Halls on Students: The Research." In D. DeCoster and P. Mable (Eds.), *Student Personnel and Education in College Residence Halls.* Cincinnati, Ohio: American College Personnel Association, 1974.

Linda Pedretty Rowe founded and chaired The Task Force on Living Learning Centers of Commission III, American College Personnel Association (ACPA). Previously, she was coordinator for residence life at the living learning center at Indiana University, Bloomington. She is currently a homemaker and mother of two pre-school children in Huntington, West Virginia, and serves on the Directorate Body of ACPA's Commission III.

Competent staff are vital in achieving the goals of residential education. To get good staff, administrators must learn how to wisely choose among applicants.

Selecting Competent Residence Hall Staff

D. David Ostroth

Many candidates for entry-level student affairs positions will be surprised to learn that staffing is one of the toughest problems for most administrators in the field. In residence hall administration this is particularly true because of high staff turnover. Even if applicants are equal in competencies, it is a real challenge to judge those competencies accurately and to match the right people to the right jobs. Effective staff selection may well determine the difference between success and failure in a residence life program.

In the 1980s and beyond, it will not be enough for residence halls to merely provide basic student needs. Rather, residence halls must increasingly provide an educational environment as an integral part of the central teaching function of the college. The goals of an educational community demand staff with a deep professional commitment. Both resident assistants and professionals will need a broad range of skills, from competencies in practical administrative detail to the more sophisticated aspects of instruction, consultation, and milieu management. The advent of student development philosophy has placed increased emphasis on professional competence. Crookston (1972) terms the new approach "competency oriented," emphasizing the value of staff abilities over status based merely on position titles. Competent staff are clearly a primary resource in the development of an educational community experience in residence halls.

Overview of Staff Selection

Selection is typically viewed as a process of matching candidate and job characteristics to predict job success (Beatty and Schneier, 1977; Glueck, 1978; Miner and Miner, 1977; Schneider, 1976). Because residence hall work involves so many functions, the prediction of success in these diverse tasks is a complex challenge for the selector. Schneider (1976) sees hiring as a two-way process in which both candidate and organizational needs must be satisfied. Predictions of candidate success involve elements of change, but the selector will make fewer incorrect predictions if a systematic approach is taken (Denerly and Plumbley, 1969).

Lopez (1965) suggests the following selection strategy: (1) assess the applicant; (2) evaluate the applicant's qualifications by comparison to a pre-determined specification of qualities needed; (3) predict the applicant's probable job success; and (4) decide whether or not to hire the applicant. Figure 1 presents a more extensive illustration of selection steps.

A careful job analysis should be the first step in any selection process. One purpose of this analysis is to clearly specify, in writing, the characteristics to be sought in candidates. Studies have repeatedly demonstrated that selection results are better when the selector knows a great deal about the job and about the kinds of people who succeed in it (Miner and Miner, 1977). O'Leary (1976) suggests that, in defining the qualities wanted, it may be helpful to interview those who have held the position in question. Denerly and Plumbley (1969) classify candidate attributes as (1) essential attributes, indispensable to satisfactory performance; (2) desirable attributes, which are less essential but preferred; and (3) contraindicators, which would disqualify a candidate. In preparing a job specification (that part of a job description listing the competencies needed for success), attention should be given to all three of these categories. One excellent source of ideas for the job specification is the detailed American College Personnel Association's (ACPA) taxonomy of student development staff skills and competencies (Hanson, 1976).

The second major step in the selection process is to develop a pool of candidates for the position. Selectivity can only be exercised when the candidate pool substantially exceeds the number of positions available. Professional

Figure 1. Components of the Selection Process

Identify Qualities Wanted	*Recruit a Pool of Candidates*	*Gather Candidate Information*	*Combine Data to Make Decision*
Assess job	Advertisement	Correspondence	
Specify	Correspondence	Resumé	
essentials,	Conferences	Application blank	
desirables, and		Interview(s)	
contraindicators		References	
		Phone calls	

positions are typically advertised through national media such as the *Chronicle of Higher Education* or the American Personnel and Guidance Association *Guidepost;* professional organizations provide excellent recruiting services through their national conferences. Recruiting for paraprofessional positions depends far more on the public relations of the residence hall program. If students perceive resident assistant positions as rewarding, it will not be difficult to generate an applicant pool.

As a pool of candidates is recruited, the selector must gather relevant information for use in making hiring decisions. The actuarial method (centered on the results of tests and other diagnostic tools) and the clinical method (centered on interviewer judgment) are two approaches to selection discussed in the literature. The interview tends to play a central role in selection for residence hall staff. However, research reveals that this "clinical" approach is subject to various sources of error: (1) interviewer stereotypes and biases may heavily influence outcomes; (2) unfavorable candidate information may not be given too much weight, especially if the interviewer is under pressure to hire; (3) interviewers may not persist in gathering new information once their biases appear to be supported; and (4) first impressions may excessively influence selection decisions (Webster, 1964).

The Role of Affirmative Action

No discussion on staff selection can be complete without consideration of equal opportunity and affirmative action requirements. Title VII of the Civil Rights Act of 1964 (amended in 1972 to include employees of educational institutions) forbids discrimination on the basis of race, sex, religion, or national origin in any type of personnel decision. The 1972 Equal Employment Opportunity Act granted the Equal Employment Opportunity Commission (EEOC) power to take companies or institutions to court. This fact, along with the court cases and consent decrees which followed it, have significantly increased the effectiveness of EEOC compliance efforts. Employers are expected to take affirmative action to remedy imbalances in race or sex that may be due to past discrimination in hiring.

The law in this area has been developing actively and will continue to change in the years ahead. The landmark case of *Griggs* v. *Duke Power Co.* established the principle that employment practices having the *effect* of discrimination are illegal even if the employer did not *intend* to discriminate. Subsequent cases have modified and further developed this principle. Staff selection procedures are legal regardless of their effect if the employer can show they relate directly to the requirements of the job.

EEOC regulations have established guidelines for questions that may and may not be asked in selection interviews. In general, it is illegal to ask questions about an applicant's birthplace, age, religion, race, citizenship, or arrest record. An employer may not ask for a photograph of a candidate before hiring. Questions are generally legal if they establish job-related information, that is, if the answers will tell the selector information which helps predict success for the particular job in question.

Equal opportunity and affirmative action have become increasingly complex areas of regulation and law. Selectors should consult their institution's affirmative action officer regularly for guidance on hiring procedures. It is important to advertise professional positions widely for the broadest possible candidate pool. In addition to affirmative action benefits, advertising will help the employer develop a diversified candidate pool with the variety of competencies so vulnerable in developing a healthy educational environment in residence halls.

Reliability and Validity of Selection Procedures

The field of personnel psychology has produced significant research on the reliability and validity of various methods of gathering information about job candidates. The *reliability* of a selection technique may be defined as the consistency with which that technique gathers candidate information and leads to conclusions based on consistent information. *Validity* is the degree to which a selection technique gathers accurate candidate information and leads to accurate predictions of job success. The findings on selection tools often used in student affairs are summarized below.

The Resumé and Application Blank. The resumé often provides a biased and unreliable view of an applicant and should be considered suspect (Gaudet and Casey, 1959). Very little research has been reported validating the usefulness of the resumé. Application blanks can provide more controlled information for screening and personnel uses (Lopez, 1965). If application blanks are used in selection decisions, each item should be weighed for its validity in helping to predict subsequent employee success. More detailed "biographical information blanks," when validated against performance criteria, may be useful in making short-term predictions of candidate success (Schneider, 1976).

The Written Recommendation. Written references have been found unreliable as selection tools. Judges have been found to disagree as to the value of the same reference letters (Rim, 1976). The validity of "Objectively" scaled references has also been shown to be generally low and to vary depending on the writer (Browning, 1968; Mosel and Goheen, 1958; 1959). References often apply adjectives to applicants rather than giving specifics; different kinds of adjectives may vary in their discrimination between good and poor applicants (Peres and Garcia, 1962). Authors strongly recommend that references be corroborated through personal telephone contacts with the writers (Mandell, 1958; Miner, 1977). By interviewing people who know the candidate, one can obtain information (particularly very negative information) that is not otherwise available (Goheen and Mosel, 1959).

The Selection Interview. Research has shown numerous ways in which the interview may be unreliable and/or invalid (Kahn and Cannell, 1957; Dunnette, 1966; Taylor, 1972; Carlson, and others, 1974). Much of the difficulty with interviews arises from unreliability, that is, inconsistency in the information gathered and in the resulting hiring decisions. When more than one person conducts interviews for the same position, reliability is especially low unless the interview is structured and interviewers agree on what information is important (Mayfield, 1964; Mayfield and Carlson, 1966). First impressions, even those based on written material, can heavily influence the evaluation of a candidate.

Despite some of these difficulties, the selection interview can be done effectively and can serve purposes other than information-gathering. Interviews can reveal the whole candidate, allow for detailed two-way information exchange, and enable the employer to observe candidates' appearance and oral communication skills.

To summarize research on the selection interview, four main recommendations may be suggested for interviewing practice: (1) Interviews should be planned with some degree of structure, because this approach will yield a more reliable result than is possible with unstructured interviews (Carlson and others, 1974; Ulrich and Trumbo, 1965). (2) Notes should be taken, preferably with the use of a written interview guide, since otherwise interviewer memory is not reliable (Carlson and others, 1974). (3) Interviewers should receive systematic skill training in order to maximize the validity of their conclusions based on interviews (Carlson and others, 1971; Miner, 1977; Schneider, 1976). (4) To avoid bias due to first impressions, interviewers should *not* review written information on candidates before interviews (Miner, 1977; Webster, 1964).

Selecting Undergraduate Staff

Most residence hall programs rely on the services of undergraduate resident assistants (RAs) to provide primary services. The functions of RAs are many, ranging from enforcing rules and maintaining the physical plant to advising, peer counseling, and teaching study habits (Hoyt and Davidson, 1967). As the goals of residence programs become more oriented to student development, RA functions probably will become more varied (Wyrick and Mitchell, 1971). One difficulty in identifying effective selection practices in this area has been the varied (and often vague) definitions of RA roles (Atkinson and others, 1973). Another has been the differences in viewpoint on evaluation of effectiveness; success of the RA may be viewed quite differently by the supervisors in residence programs and in physical plant management (Hoyt and Davidson, 1967). A key element in RA selection strategy, therefore, is the careful definition of job expectations, desired competencies, and evaluation criteria. Unless an effective program of staff evaluation exists, it is impossible to systematically relate selection practices to their consequences in staff performance.

Traditional procedures for RA selection have included application forms, interviews, and references (Schroeder and Willis, 1973). Grades and experiences with cocurricular activities are usually considered. Both individual and panel interviews are common; professional staff and paraprofessionals often serve as interviewers (Correnti and Tuttle, 1972). However, these standard approaches have not always been successful in predicting RA effectiveness (Graff and Bradshaw, 1970).

Since the mid 1960s, a number of researchers have investigated various other techniques in RA selection. Newer selection techniques have been proposed to supplement or even supplant traditional approaches. Among these new techniques are peer ratings, role playing, the leaderless group discussion, and apprenticeships.

Peer Ratings. Tibbits (1977) had RA applicants rate each other anonymously on ability to perform specified tasks. After testing in three different settings using small numbers of subjects, Tibbits found that peer ratings would have resulted in selection decisions almost identical to those made by more costly methods. In a related approach, Wotruba and Crawley (1967) found the results of a sociometric questionnaire quite effective in predicting RA selections made by conventional interview methods. Thus peer ratings may be a more economical (though not necessarily a more valid) method of RA selection than the traditional interview.

Role Playing. In this technique, RA candidates act out hypothetical job-related situations posed by the selection staff. Raters observe the performances and evaluate the communication and problem-solving skills demonstrated by the candidates. The advantage of this approach is that selectors may view a sample of job-related behavior and evaluate it without the need to participate actively. In studies by Sheeder (1963) and Nair and Sonders (1969), both staff and candidates responded positively to role playing as a selection procedure. Although role playing has been satisfying to participants, it is uncertain whether candidates selected this way perform better than those selected under conventional interviewing procedures.

The Leaderless Group Discussion *(LGD)*. The LGD (Bass, 1949) is a third selection procedure which shows promising results. In this approach, a small group of applicants is given one or more discussion topics. Professional staff then observe the discussion and usually take notes rating the participants. Brady (1955) found the LGD valuable for its economical use of staff time. He also observed that candidate self-consciousness (a problem in the typical interview) is reduced through the LGD, so that candidates behave more naturally. Banta and McCormick (1969) and Mullozzi and Spees (1971) also endorse the LGD in RA selection. However, in the only predictive study on the LGD, Haldane (1973) could not identify a significant correlation between LGD ratings and job performance. In summary, the LGD has been found satisfactory as a selection procedure, but its predictive validity has not been shown.

Apprenticeships and Courses. Correnti and Tuttle (1972) used a six-week apprenticeship program as a selection tool. RA candidates received presentations and participated in small group discussions on topics of concern to RAs. Candidates were rated throughout the apprenticeship by professionals and current RAs; participants also evaluated each other at the end of the program. The apprenticeship was a valuable selection procedure that offered candidates and selectors more time to evaluate their decisions. This approach is also valuable because it permits selectors to observe a wider range of job-related candidate behavior over an extended period. This eliminates some of the bias that may be inherent in a brief interview.

In addition to the above techniques, a number of personality inventories have been studied as aids to RA selection. Although a number of *concurrent* studies have been reported, relatively few studies have investigated the *predictive* validity of inventories in identifying candidates who will be successful. These predictive studies often have yielded disappointing results (Atkinson and others, 1973; Correnti and Tuttle, 1972). Research findings on a few frequently studied instruments are summarized below.

Standardized Tests:

The California Personality Inventory (CPI): Morton (1975–1976) found relationships between some CPI personality-trait scores and RA effectiveness as judged by supervisors. Dorin (1974) identified different groups of CPI subscales that predicted male and female RA performance. Ball (1977) found that the CPI subscales for Flexibility and Achievement via Independence were related to RA effectiveness. Hall and Creed (1979) compared CPI scores of practicing RAs with those of a random control group; the RAs scored significantly higher on five of six scales describing interpersonal adequacy. On the other hand, research by Dolan (1965), Schroeder and Dowse (1968), and Haldane (1973) did not find the CPI useful for selection.

The Personal Orientation Inventory (POI): Mullozzi and Spees (1971) found one POI scale that added slightly to the prediction of candidate success as a resident fellow. Studies by Atkinson and others (1973) and Schroeder and Willis (1973) do not support the value of the POI. However, Graff and Bradshaw (1970) found four POI scales related to RA effectiveness as rated by residents and student affairs deans. Anthony (1973) found the POI Self-Acceptance scale correlated with the effectiveness of female student assistants. Kipp (1979) found candidates selected by traditional methods to be significantly more self-actualized, as measured by the POI, than those rejected. Based on these conflicting findings, it appears that POI results vary with the situation in which the instrument is used.

The Myers-Briggs Type Indicator (MBTI): The relation between MBTI scores and RA effectiveness was explored by Wachowiak and Bauer (1977). Accepted RA applicants were less perception-oriented than those rejected. Student evaluations of their RAs were unrelated to MBTI scores, but RAs with lower Sensing-Intuiting scores were more positively rated by their head residents.

The Authoritarian F Scale: Hoyt and Davidson (1967) found that ineffective RAs (as rated by Head Counselors) tended to receive more authoritarian F scores than did effective RAs. Some additional support for the Authoritarian F Scale (used for selection in conjunction with other instruments) was given by Bodden and Walsh (1968).

Although some instruments show promise, no single instrument or group of instruments has consistently demonstrated predictive validity in a variety of settings. Results often varied with the sex and job expectations of the subjects studied.

In summary, the effective selection of RAs depends on a clear statement of the job functions the RA will perform and the competencies the RA will need to perform them. Criteria for performance evaluation should be established, and the performance of those hired should be related back to selection procedures that produced accurate predictions. Grades and activities indicative of leadership skills will probably remain among the best predictors of success in resident assistants. Interviews should have structure, and rating criteria should be understood in advance by well-trained interviewers. Peer nomination of RA candidates is one method of identifying promising applicants.

Among the new techniques, the leaderless group discussion is probably the most satisfactory; it saves staff time and allows candidates to be more natural during evaluation. More research is needed, however, to determine the validity of this procedure in identifying the most successful candidates. If extensive preservice training is feasible within a residence hall program, administrators should consider an apprenticeship program where selection is contingent on successful performance in training. Apprenticeship may be an expensive and time-consuming procedure, but it is probably the most valid because it allows a much deeper look at a candidate's competencies and weaknesses.

At present, research findings do not appear to support the value of any standardized instrument as a major tool for predicting success of RAs. Of the available instruments the CPI and the POI show the greatest potential as aids to staff selection. Research on these and other inventories should continue, with the use of clear job definitions and standardized performance ratings in a predictive rather than concurrent measurement design. For the present, administrators wishing to use inventories in RA selection should rely on their own findings based on local norms.

Selecting Professional Staff

Despite the extensive literature on RA selection reviewed above, there has been very little research published on the selection of professionals in student affairs. The literature in this area consists mostly of job market surveys and post-conference placement evaluations. The lack of research on professional staff selection is a significant omission in the literature.

As a beginning step in such research, this investigator mailed surveys to student affairs administrators who selected entry-level professional staff in 1978. Two main questions were addressed in this study: (1) What, in the opinion of the selectors, were the competencies desired in entry-level candidates? (2) What selection techniques are commonly in use in student affairs?

The population for this study included all administrators named as "contact persons" (to whom application is made) in job listings for entry-level positions advertised during the 1978 ACPA, National Association for Women Deans, Administrators, and Counselors, and National Association of Student Personnel Administrators conferences. Entry-level professional positions were defined as those for which a related master's degree was required or desired and not more than one year's related experience was required. After duplicate job listings were eliminated, 111 head resident or residence staff positions were identified. A questionnaire was mailed to a random sample of 56 contact persons; a total of 55 (98.2 percent) returned usable responses (Ostroth, 1981).

Competencies Desired in Professionals. The questionnaire asked each respondent to rate the importance of thirty-six specific competencies as criteria used in selection for a particular position named on the form. The competency statements used in this study were derived from research by Minetti (1977). The key question asked of respondents was, "In selecting the best candidate for the position named in the questionnaire, how important was each of the competencies listed, in your opinion?" Each competency was rated on a five point scale, from "absolutely essential" (a candidate had to have this competency to be considered for the position) to "of no importance" (this competency is unimportant in the job; it was not a factor in judging candidates).

Table 1 shows the competencies rated either "absolutely essential" or "very important" by at least 60 percent of the respondents. Although the ability to assess student needs and interests is rated very highly in this format, only 47.3 percent of the respondents found this competency essential. Three other competencies were rated "absolutely essential" by much larger proportions of respondents: "Work cooperatively with others" (80 percent), "Work effectively with a wide range of individuals" (74.5 percent), and "Manifest well-developed interpersonal relations and communication skills" (70.9 percent). Other general competencies which were highly rated include leadership ability and decision-making skills. Employers identified a number of more specific competencies as important; these include expertise in conflict mediation and discipline, programming skills, and competencies in staff supervision and group advisement.

The competencies rated relatively lowest in importance in this study included psychometric skills, statistical and research expertise, political acumen, and financial/budgeting skills. Overall, it appears that employers are seeking staff with basic personality traits and general abilities that will enable them to function in practical ways. Highly specific skills and knowledge were rated as somewhat less important than general abilities—particularly competencies in interpersonal communication, leadership, decision-making, and working cooperatively with a wide range of people.

Table 1. Ratings of the Most Important Competencies

The candidate should have the ability to:	Percent of Respondents Rating the Competency "Absolutely Essential" or "Very Important"
Assess student needs and interests	94.6
Work effectively with a wide range of individuals	94.5
Work cooperatively with others	92.7
Manifest well-developed interpersonal relations and communication skills	90.9
Display leadership skills	90.9
Mediate conflicts between individuals and groups	90.9
Engage in effective decision-making	89.1
Perform fair and effective discipline of student misconduct	87.3
Meet student developmental needs through cocurricular programs and activities	83.7
Select, train, supervise, and evaluate staff	80.0
Advise groups	78.2
Appreciate and internalize professional standards and ethics	76.4
Recognize and evaluate group dynamics	71.0
Represent student concerns to other campus populations	63.6
Display competence in individual and group counseling	63.6
Appreciate and understand the specialized functions of student personnel work	63.6
Recognize and interpret the special needs of ethnic and racial minorities	61.8
Interpret to students the concerns, goals, and problems of the other campus populations	60.0

Procedures to Select Professionals. In the same study, employers were asked specific questions concerning the procedures they used in selecting staff for the named entry-level positions. Relevant findings can be summarized as follows:

1. Almost all the respondents had a written job description they reviewed when filling the position.
2. Only 72 percent had a written specification of the qualifications candidates would need; these specifications were less detailed than the literature suggests they should be.
3. Less than one-fourth of the respondents used application blanks; only one used a personality inventory.
4. Almost 95 percent contacted the writers of references for candidates under serious consideration.
5. Nearly 90 percent of the responding employers did some conference interviewing. Over two thirds used more than one interviewer, but only 6 percent conducted formal interviewer training.
6. Responses indicated that conference interviews are not as structured as recommended in the literature: less than one-fourth of the respondents used written interview guides.

7. Almost all respondents took notes in conjunction with conference interviews (usually *after* the interviews), but only 38 percent used established rating forms.
8. Interviewers read written information on candidates before interviews in over 90 percent of the cases.

The above data show that many employers could improve their selection of residence professionals by applying research findings to their selection strategies.

General Recommendations for Valid Selection

Selection of residence hall staff (whether professional or paraprofessional) can become a burden: it can be repetitive, time-consuming, and tedious. Yet the importance of the outcomes of selection cannot be overestimated. Clearly this is an area which calls for close professional attention. Here are some suggestions for the "nuts and bolts" of selection:

Planning. Each time there are positions to be filled, the selection strategy and time line should be carefully planned. Commitments and suggestions should be obtained from staff members who are to participate in the selection program. Clear procedures for the maintenance of files and the tracking of candidates should be established. A haphazard selection process may lead to candidate and staff dissatisfaction, as well as invalid hiring decisions.

Affirmative Action. Employers should determine EEO compliance requirements by checking with their institutional professionals in this area. Plans should be established for keeping the appropriate records and reporting the necessary statistics. All recruiting materials should be reviewed for compliance with EEO guidelines. Recruiting and advertising should be planned to attract the broadest possible pool of qualified candidates.

Advertising. In addition to the above, advertisements should accurately reflect the job content and responsibilities. Consideration should be given to stating the salary range for professional positions, rather than leaving it vague.

To recruit a broadly-based candidate pool, employers should consider contacting professional colleagues and graduate training programs, in addition to posting advertisements nationally. Sources of qualified minority candidates should be aggressively sought.

Job Analysis and Description. Before launching a selection process, the employer should thoroughly review the written job description. Staff currently holding the job in question should be asked for suggestions in revising the job description. The revised job description should be duplicated and distributed to candidates. Remember that selection is a two-way process; the job description should be specific enough to give candidates accurate and complete information about the position. As an integral part of the job analysis and description, the selector should specify the competencies needed for the position. This specification will be most helpful if it details in writing the essential and desirable candidate characteristics, as well as factors that would disqualify a candidate. All staff members who are to participate in selection should be aware of these criteria.

Correspondence. In preparing for selection, all correspondence should be reviewed. Any inappropriate sexist language should be removed. Correspondence should be designed to minimize response delays and expense. In all but the largest selection programs, mimeographed form letters should be eliminated if possible. Candidates appreciate individualized correspondence; a good approach is to record letters on a mag card or memory typewriter.

Convention Selection Activities. National professional conferences are good places for recruiting and screening a strong, varied candidate pool. Conference recruiting can be hectic, so it is best to schedule interviews in advance. Conference procedures should be planned in detail. Forms for corresponding with candidates will save note writing. If an interview team is used, the team should meet ahead of time and agree on common procedures and selection criteria. Time should be allowed in the interview schedule to see outstanding candidates who may not come forward until the conference.

Follow-up with Candidates. Whether or not conference interviews are done, procedures are needed to track candidates through the selection process. There should be a strong commitment to keep candidates appraised of their status as decisions are made. Those who are rejected should be notified at once. Rejection letters must be carefully worded; the ideal letter states the facts simply, clearly, and considerately, without confusing or long-winded euphemisms.

Decision-Making. The process of making hiring decisions will be simpler and more valid if good criteria have been established and applied throughout the selection process. A team approach is helpful in assessing different aspects of candidate qualifications. Remember that a variety of different personalities, with variation in some competencies, can make for a better-rounded and more creative staff.

Selection Techniques

In addition to the above recommendations, selection research points to a number of conclusions for maximizing the reliability and validity of selection techniques:

The Resumé and Application Blank. Although the resumé may contain a good deal of useful information, remember that it is unreliable because candidates may shade the data they include in different ways. The application blank has interesting potential as a selection tool. Employers should consider developing weighted application blanks whose items are validated for prediction of relevant success criteria. Miner and Miner (1977) describe a simple "horizontal percent" method for weighting application blank items as selection predictors. To apply this method, the employer needs a staff evaluation that divides staff at the median for effectiveness on the job. Because of its simplicity, the horizontal percent technique holds promise for residence programs that hire a number of people annually.

The Reference. Again, employers should recognize that references may be unreliable because they are often vague and because people attach different values to the same statements. One study (Peres and Garcia, 1962) showed that adjectives describing candidates as "nice people" are less discriminating than those describing candidates' mental agility. The most important recommendation is that selectors validate references by interviewing or telephoning the writers.

The Selection Interview. The objectives of selection interviews should be carefully defined by employers. The semistructured or unstructured interview serves to assess a candidate's communication skills and to explore personality in a two-way exchange. However, those interviews designed primarily to gather information to screen candidates should be more structured than they often are. For these interviews, employers should develop written interview guides containing questions to be asked of all candidates. This guide is especially helpful when there is more than one interviewer; otherwise, different interviewers may seek different information, and the results may vary. To increase the reliability of interviews, interviewers should use a standard candidate rating form and take notes during interviews. If this is impossible, notes and written evaluations should be completed immediately following interviews. When more than one staff person is to be involved in selection, the employer should consider formally training staff in interview techniques and the realistic use of written candidate information. Before or during such training, all involved staff should reach consensus on the qualities to be sought in candidates and on the methods of evaluating those qualities. The literature suggests that it may be desirable for interviewers *not* to review written information on candidates prior to selection interviews. It may be effective to have one staff member screen written information and arrange for interviews by another staff member.

Conclusions

The overview of selection presented here indicates that a "scientific" or systematic approach can make residence staff selection more effective. The research indicates that, in several areas, procedural improvements are needed. Yet there seems to be no proof that selection is solely a structured and objective process. The use of procedures having established reliability and validity can reduce uncertainty in making predictions of candidate success. However, in selecting staff for the multifaceted roles of residence hall workers, a significant judgment factor always remains. To this extent, staff selection in residence life is undoubtedly an art as well as a science.

Baier (1979) points out that, when student affairs organizations are competently staffed, they remain viable and innovative even during periods of fiscal retrenchment. Competent and innovative staff are needed to develop a supportive community environment and to maximize the educational value of the student residential experience. This makes selection of staff a vital process in the service of these goals.

References

Anthony, V. L. "Personality Correlates of Effectiveness Among Student Assistants in Residence Halls." Unpublished doctoral dissertation, Oklahoma State University, 1973.

Atkinson, D. R., Williams, T. D., and Garb, E. "The Personal Orientation Inventory as a Predictor of Resident Assistant Effectiveness." *Journal of College Student Personnel,* 1973, *14,* 326–332.

Baier, J. L. "Competent Staff: The Critical Variable." In M. J. Barr and L. A. Keating (Eds.), *New Directions for Student Services: Establishing Effective Programs,* no. 7. San Francisco: Jossey-Bass, 1979.

Ball, W. D. "An Investigation of the Relationship Between Resident Assistant Effectiveness at Mississippi State University and Personal Characteristics as Measured by the California Psychological Inventory." Unpublished doctoral dissertation, Mississippi State University, 1977.

Banta, T. W., and McCormick, J. E. "Using the Leaderless Group Discussion Technique for the Selection of Residence Hall Counselors." *Journal of the National Association for Women Deans and Counselors,* Fall 1969, *33,* 30–33.

Bass, B. M. "An Analysis of the Leaderless Group Discussion." *Journal of Applied Psychology,* 1949, *33,* 527–533.

Beatty, R. W., and Schneier, C. E. *Personnel Administration: An Experiential/Skill-Building Approach.* Reading, Mass.: Addison-Wesley, 1977.

Bodden, J. L., and Walsh, W. B. "Increasing the Effectiveness of the Selection of Residence Counselors." *Journal of College Student Personnel,* 1968, *9,* 193–194.

Brady, M. V. "Student Counselor Selection." *Personnel and Guidance Journal,* 1955, *33,* 289–292.

Browning, R. C. "Validity of Reference Ratings from Previous Employers." *Personnel Psychology,* 1968, *21,* 389–393.

Carlson, R. E., Thayer, P. W., Mayfield, E. C., and Peterson, D. A. "Improvements in the Selection Interview." *Personnel Journal,* 1971, *50,* 268–275, 317.

Carlson, R. E., Thayer, P. W., Mayfield, E. C., and Peterson, D. A. "Research on the Selection Interview." In E. A. Fleishman and A. R. Bass (Eds.), *Studies in Personnel and Industrial Psychology.* Homewood, Ill.: Dorsey Press, 1974.

Correnti, R. J., and Tuttle, C. E. "An Apprenticeship Program for Resident Assistants." *NASPA Journal,* 1972, *10,* 132–137.

Crookston, B. B. "An Organizational Model for Student Development." *NASPA Journal,* 1972, *10,* 3–13.

Denerly, R. A., and Plumbley, P. R. *Recruitment and Selection in a Full-Employment Economy.* London: Institute of Personnel Management, 1969.

Dolan, F. A. "Personal Qualities and Characteristics Important in the Selection of Undergraduate Staff Members for Women's Residence Halls." Unpublished doctoral dissertation, Northwestern University, 1965.

Dorin, P. A. "The Use of the California Psychological Inventory in the Selection of Residence Hall Staff." Unpublished doctoral dissertation, University of Connecticut, 1974.

Dunnette, M. D. *Personnel Selection and Placement.* Belmont, Calif.: Wadsworth, 1966.

Gaudet, F. J., and Casey, T. F. "How Much Can You Tell from a Resumé?" *Personnel,* 1959, *36,* 62–65.

Glueck, W. F. *Personnel: A Diagnostic Approach.* Dallas: Business Publications, 1978.

Goheen, H. W., and Mosel, J. N. "Validity of Employment Recommendation Questionnaire: II. Comparison with Field Investigations." *Personnel Psychology*, 1959, *12*, 300–308.

Graff, R. W., and Bradshaw, H. E. "Relationship of a Measure of Self-Actualization to Dormitory Resident Assistant Effectiveness." *Journal of Counseling Psychology*, 1970, *17*, 502–505.

Griggs v. *Duke Power Co.*, 401 U.S. 424 (1971).

Haldane, M. B. "Leaderless Group Discussion Method as an Effective Procedure for Selection of Residence Hall Counselors." Unpublished doctoral dissertation, Northwestern University, 1973.

Hall, M., and Creed, W. "The Use of the CPI in the Evaluation and Selection of Resident Assistants." *Journal of College and University Student Housing*, 1979, *9*, 10–13.

Hanson, G. "Tentative Taxonomy of Student Development Staff Skills and Competencies." Unpublished manuscript, American College Personnel Association, 1976. (Available from Gary Hanson, Assistant Dean of Students, University of Texas, Austin, Tex. 78712.)

Hoyt, D. P., and Davidson, A. "Evaluating Residence Hall Advisers." *Journal of College Student Personnel*, 1967, *8*, 251–256.

Kahn, R. L., and Cannell, C. F. *The Dynamics of Interviewing.* New York: Wiley, 1957.

Kipp, D. J. "The Personal Orientation Inventory: A Predictive Device for Resident Advisers." *Journal of College Student Personnel*, 1979, *20*, 382–384.

Lopez, F. M., Jr. *Personnel Interviewing.* New York: McGraw-Hill, 1965.

Mandell, M. M. "Checking References: How to Get the Facts." *Supervisory Management*, 1958, *3*(3), 10–17.

Mayfield, E. C. "The Selection Interview—A Reevaluation of Published Research." *Personnel Psychology*, 1964, *17*, 239–260.

Mayfield, E. C., and Carlson, R. E. "Selection Interview Decisions: First Results from a Long-Term Research Project." *Personnel Psychology*, 1966, *19*, 41–53.

Miner, J. B. "The Selection Interview." In W. C. Hamner and F. L. Schmidt (Eds.), *Contemporary Problems in Personnel.* (rev. ed.) Chicago: St. Clair Press, 1977.

Miner, J. B., and Miner, M. G. *Personnel and Industrial Relations: A Managerial Approach.* (3rd ed.). New York: Macmillan, 1977.

Minetti, R. H. "An Analytical Description of the Relationship Between the Academic Training and Assistantship Experiences of Master's Degree Programs in Student Personnel Administration." Unpublished doctoral dissertation, Michigan State University, 1977.

Morton, L. J. "The CPI: Significance as a Resident Assistant Selection Aid." *Journal of College and University Student Housing*, 1975–1976, *5*, 16–21.

Mosel, J. N., and Goheen, H. W. "The Validity of the Employment Recommendation Questionnaire in Personnel Selection." *Personnel Psychology*, 1958, *11*, 481–490.

Mosel, J. N., and Goheen, H. W. "The Employment Recommendation Questionnaire: III. Validity of Different Types of References." *Personnel Psychology*, 1959, *12*, 469–477.

Mullozzi, A., Jr., and Spees, E. R. "Factors in Selecting Residence Hall Fellows." *Journal of the National Association of Women Deans and Counselors*, 1971, *34*, 185–190.

Nair, D. A., and Sonders, O. L. "Sociodrama in the Selection and Training of Male Student Residence Hall Advisers." *NAPSA Journal*, 1969, *7*, 81–85.

O'Leary, L. R. *Interviewing for the Decisionmaker.* Chicago: Nelson-Hall, 1976.

Ostroth, D. D. "Competencies for Entry-Level Professionals: What Do Employers Look for in Hiring New Staff?" *Journal of College Student Personnel*, 1981, *22*, in press.

Peres, S. H., and Garcia, J. R. "Validity and Dimensions of Descriptive Adjectives Used in Reference Letters for Engineering Applicants." *Personnel Psychology*, 1962, *15*, 270–286.

Rim, Y. "How Reliable Are Letters of Recommendation?" *Journal of Higher Education*, 1976, *47*, 437–445.

Schneider, B. *Staffing Organizations*. Santa Monica, Calif.: Goodyear, 1976.

Schroeder, C. C., and Willis, B. S. "An Attempt to Use a Measure of Self-Actualization in the Selection of Resident Assistants." *The Journal of College and University Student Housing*, January 1973, *3*, 30–32.

Schroeder, P., and Dowse, E. "Selection, Function, and Assessment of Residence Hall Counselors." *Personnel and Guidance Journal*, 1968, *47*, 151–156.

Sheeder, W. B. "Role Playing as a Method of Selecting Dormitory Counselors." *Journal of College Student Personnel*, 1963, *4*, 154–158.

Taylor, V. R. "A Hard Look at the Selection Interview." In H. J. Chruden and A. W. Sherman, Jr. (Eds.), *Readings in Personnel Management*. Cincinnati: South-Western Publishing, 1972.

Tibbits, S. "Student Staff Selectors: Peer Evaluations May Be Best." *NASPA Journal*, 1977, *14*, 65–68.

Ulrich, L., and Trumbo, D. "The Selection Interview since 1949." *Psychological Bulletin*, 1965, *63*, 100–116.

Wachowiak, D., and Bauer, G. "Use of the Myers-Briggs Type Indicator for the Selection and Evaluation of Residence Hall Advisers." *Journal of College and University Student Housing*, Winter 1977, *6*, 34–37.

Webster, E. C. *Decision Making in the Employment Interview*. Montreal: Eagle Publishing, 1964.

Wotruba, R. T., and Crawley, W. J. "A Sociometric Questionnaire as a Guide to Select Resident Assistants." Paper presented at national conference of the American Personnel and Guidance Association, Dallas, 1967.

Wyrick, T. J., and Mitchell, K. N. "Relationship Between Resident Assistants' Empathy and Warmth and Their Effectiveness." *Journal of College Student Personnel*, 1971, *12*, 36–40.

D. David Ostroth is associate director of student development services at Virginia Polytechnic Institute and State University. He has conducted extensive research on staff selection and has been responsible for selecting residence hall staff at Michigan State University. He has held various administrative responsibilities at several universities.

This chapter presents a systematic approach to the
training of resident assistants. It suggests major categories of training,
recommends various training techniques, and provides resources
to be used in staff training.

Staff Training

John H. Schuh

Staff training is an essential element of any residence hall program. Greenleaf (1974) strongly supports the concept of a training program for student assistants: "Inservice preparation is . . . the means by which the student staff member is given an opportunity to develop knowledge and skills necessary to carry out the job responsibilities" (p. 189). However, although there may be general agreement that having student staff members is desirable, there is considerable disagreement as to the training that these staff members should receive (Powell, 1974).

    This chapter has several purposes. The first is to present general staff training categories. These categories include operational services, institutional support services, human relations skills, and programming/advising skills. The second purpose is to provide residence hall administrators with a variety of training options. One of the most difficult aspects of planning staff training is to choose from the variety of training models available and to tailor them to meet the needs of individual staff members in particular campus settings. The third purpose of the chapter is to present some thoughts and suggestions about structuring a staff training program. These ideas will appear throughout the chapter. Since so many different training components are available, it can be difficult to plan an effective training program.

    Perhaps it would be useful to offer a word about the terms *training* and *education.* In the context of this chapter, the terms are used interchangeably. However, the reader is cautioned that other authors draw more distinct differences between the two terms (Delworth and Yarris, 1978). In this chapter, *staff training* refers to the training of undergraduate and graduate student staff members, commonly referred to as resident assistants, resident advisers, or student assistants. This chapter will not address the training of professional staff members nor the training of allied staff members, such as campus ministers. For a discussion of training for these individuals, see Delworth (1978) and Delworth and Aulepp (1976).

Planning Staff Training

Many training topics will be suggested in this chapter, and obviously not all the material could be covered in preschool workshops. For this reason, some thought must be given to sequencing the training process—determining what to cover in preservice training and what to leave to in-service training. That job needs to be done systematically. While some tasks must be covered in preschool workshops, some can be addressed either before or after the residence halls open. The decision of what to cover and when to cover it should be made in conjunction with some type of needs assessment to determine what skills the staff have and what skills they need to develop. The characteristics of staff, that is, academic background, work experience, and other educational experiences, should influence the planning of training activities. A staff development committee can do this work quite well; this committee also can be employed in planning in-service training. One way to approach assessment is to employ a self-administered checklist of skills. Staff complete the checklist and indicate where their skills lie and where they need work. That information should be used to plan appropriate training modules.

Some institutions conduct a spring training program after staff have been selected but before the spring term concludes. This training schedule is especially appropriate for institutions on a quarter system because staff can be selected in the winter quarter and trained in the spring quarter for the following fall. Of course, certain staff activities that resemble training occur throughout the year. But staff meetings, where business and operational questions are decided, are not staff training sessions. Staff training means special workshops, colloquia, seminars, or classes designed specifically for skill development.

Staff training should be viewed as a sequential skill building in which knowledge and skills developed early in the training form the basis for later development. For this reason the sequence in which skills are taught is very important. Before identifying the skills that staff should develop in the preservice phase of training, one should ensure that they possess competencies that make them "safe beginners" as staff members. They should have a clear understanding of the operation of the individual residence hall, including a knowledge of the procedures students follow if the residence hall is not meeting their basic needs. Staff need to be able to handle emergencies from the moment the residence hall opens, and they need to develop a basic understanding of the organization of the university, the role of the residence staff, and the purpose of student housing. These competencies are a must for even beginning staff. As in-service training begins, its goal is to supplement the skills listed above. Although needed skills may vary widely from campus to campus, most programs call for skills in the human relations and the program development areas.

Second- and third-year staff members pose a special training concern. One can assume that they have the skills necessary to conduct their jobs properly, yet if they do not participate in training sessions the team-building effect of training will be lost. There are several ways to employ experienced staff so that the training is meaningful for them and the team-building approach is not lost. One way is to use them on a staff development committee. Experienced staff can assist in the assessment of new staff members' skills and help plan the training program. Another way is to have them present training modules. They can serve as moderators when special guests are invited to conduct training, or they can conduct the training themselves. Such involvement will recognize their special skills and make them feel particularly useful in the training process. A third way is to have returning staff develop and implement the evaluation plan for each training session. It goes without saying that training components should be evaluated meticulously, and these staff can develop the forms, and checklists necessary to the evaluation plan. By employing these people in the ways mentioned above, as well as in others appropriate to individual campuses, the objectives of the training program can be met and the returning staff members can realize some real developmental gains from the experience.

One other broad area, that of the institution's perspective toward resident assistants, should be examined. Powell (1974) suggests that two questions need to be answered before training programs can be outlined. The first concerns the institution's assumptions and goals regarding students: Should student behavior be tightly controlled and regulated? The other addresses the institution's view of the resident assistant position: Are resident assistants primarily enforcers of rules? These two basic questions, and any others suggested by individual campus conditions, must be answered before planning for the training program can proceed.

Training in Residence Hall Operations

Operational services are defined as all services and activities necessary for the operation of the residence hall. Some of these services, such as custodial care, are provided by management personnel, but others might be personnel services, such as working in the "duty office." As DeCoster and Mable (1974) point out, the general objectives for college student housing can be viewed in a hierarchical structure, and levels one and two deal with facilities-oriented concerns. The residence life staff often provides many of the facilities-oriented services, especially in emergency situations after normal working hours. This aspect of staff training is critical. Errors by staff in handling these operations assignments can have lasting effects. For example, consider the problems that can arise because of mishandled master keys. The ramifications of such errors are frightening.

Housing operations are organized in a variety of ways, and the first task in this training area is to present an organizational and functional scheme to staff. Resident assistants (RAs) need to understand which departments are responsible for specific management tasks, such as food service, custodial care, building maintenance, and finances. In some situations these tasks will be subsumed under the residence life office. In other cases, they will be assigned to a housing operations department or an auxiliary services department; or they may reside in departments unto themselves. Organizational charts, directories, and statements of organizational mission are essential training tools.

Resident assistants share responsibility for accomplishing a number of these operational tasks, from arranging for special meal requests to assisting at the hall reception desk. Perhaps the easiest way to acquaint staff with responsibilities in this area is to give them a manual of sample forms, both blank and completed. Then staff members can work through a prepared set of simulated operational problems. These operational tasks must be mastered before other training is attempted since a residence hall that is not self-sustaining is not ready for students.

There are a number of basic operational skills that must be mastered by the residence life staff. These include the following: handling meal ticket problems, using master keys, checking students in and out of their rooms, handling emergency repair problems, completing a room change, handling and completing room inventory sheet, completing a maintenance repair request, working the residence hall desk, interpreting the residence hall contract, handling overnight guests of resident students, and supervising emergency evacuation of the building.

It is difficult to measure the competencies of staff in responsibly performing these necessary operations until they are on the job. Careful supervision of staff during the first several weeks of the residence hall operation is necessary to determine where weaknesses exist. If the problems that arise are common to all staff members, staff meeting time should be devoted to correcting these deficiencies. If the problems are particular to only several individuals, they should receive special training outside the staff meeting.

Training in Institutional Support Services

Residence life staff are very dependent on other campus services for support and assistance. A primary function of most residence life staffs is to advise and refer student residents to offices where they can get expert assistance. These referrals should be quick and accurate, since poor referrals result in confusion, inefficiency, and student unhappiness (Shelton and Corazzini, 1976).

Moreover, the residence life office is usually dependent on other campus services for program support. For instance career planning and placement counselors frequently visit residence halls to offer advice on making career decisions, finding summer work, or selecting a major. Many other visiting services are available, and the residence hall staff might be characterized as "campus pickpockets" because it is their job to "steal" these services for their halls and tell residents about them.

A big problem in orienting staff to campus services is that it can be overwhelming to have all of the campus support services make presentations in a preservice workshop. A list of such offices on one campus included some seventy-five support groups. To give each office time in a preservice workshop is highly unrealistic.

One way to solve this problem is to mirror the approach taken to operations functions. Like some operational procedures, some campus agencies are critical to the opening of a residence hall. These are the service agencies to introduce to staff before the halls are opened. The staff can learn of less critical services during in-service training program after the halls are opened. Among the critical services are police, fire, and health services. Whether these services are provided by the institution or local agencies, they are essential to the operation of a residence hall. Time devoted to learning about these services is time well spent. A mistake in referring a critically ill student or handling a police or fire emergency can mean loss of life or severe property damage. Such staff errors simply cannot be tolerated.

Beyond these critical services, staff will need timely training in other areas because some problems are more likely to arise earlier in the academic year than others. For example, it is unlikely that students will face immediate placement problems. However, transportation information, including parking regulations, campus bus services, and the like may be critical to new students. Staff need to know about these services, or be able to make a proper referral.

Familiarizing staff with all of the campus support offices, functions, and locations is a complex task. Having the director of each service make a short presentation to the staff is impractical and generally leads to a series of tedious lectures that fall on unattentive ears. Giving the staff a manual in the hope that RAs will read and digest the information is wishful thinking. However, there are some effective tools for introducing staff to these services—ways that will make them remember the material and enable them to make proper referrals.

One of the best ways is the campus search, similar to a scavenger hunt. Staff are given a list of offices to visit on campus. Next to the office name is a blank where the receptionist or director initials the list to prove that the staff member has found the offices. After the search is completed, the entire staff is debriefed and shares information discovered about the offices. Material in a manual can then be used to reinforce what the staff found out during the search.

Another method used to introduce staff to services is audiovisual presentations. Short slide/tape programs about each service or offices are shown to staff. Question-and-answer periods conducted by departmental representatives follow. This approach is shorter but not as effective as the campus search. The campus search can take as long as eight hours, whereas this media approach might take less than a half day.

As the academic year unfolds, it becomes important to introduce staff to other campus services. Oral and written presentations at staff meetings or staff visits to the service agency are traditional training approaches. Unfortunately, office presentations are time consuming, and oral or written presentations vary widely in quality and accuracy.

It is difficult to determine staff skill levels in making referrals. Some staff will have had frequent encounters with some offices and will be familiar with the services offered, whereas others will be less well informed. One means of determining staff familiarity with these services is to have the staff list the offices with which they believe they are conversant and answer a series of open-ended questions about them. This exericse serves as a short quiz and departure point from which to begin training. Those staff members who demonstrate competence can serve as group leaders in the campus search or discussion leaders in debriefing sessions on campus services. Do not overlook trained staff as a training resource.

There remains another facet of orienting staff to services: updating staff on new services (or new aspects of old services) that emerge during the school year. This process can be completed most efficiently through staff meetings. The new information should be a typed or printed addendum to the staff manual. Additionally, refresher sessions, held at least twice yearly during staff meetings, should review the services offered by campus agencies. To ensure appropriate referrals and the smooth operation of the residence hall, resident assistants must be familiar with services offered by campus agencies. This aspect of staff training a very important building block in the total staff development structure.

Training in Human Relations

Resident assistants need to interact skillfully with students, since an important RA function is to provide advice and counsel. One cannot deny that resident assistants have important managerial and administrative responsibilities, but they will be doomed to failure if they cannot work effectively with students.

The human relations role of RAs has grown in importance over the past several years, as Meade (1978) points out. However, merely training staff in some rudimentary interpersonal relations skills is valueless without an overall framework and definition against which to examine such training. Cursory training in human relations will not develop an acceptable level of competence in staff. They must understand why they are developing these skills, and how these skills fit into the overall training program. Moreover, simply working through some human relations training exercises and calling the process "counseling skill development" or "human relations training" is shortchanging the staff in their training program.

This section will discuss several different human relations training models and judge their applicability to resident assistant training programs. Additional training areas will be suggested as steps toward a comprehensive human relations training program for resident assistants.

Over the last dozen years a number of excellent human relations training models have been developed that can be adapted for use with resident assistants. Meade (1978) gives a particularly lucid discussion and critique of these models; Meade is an excellent source of further information about the models. The following brief discussion gives the format and resource requirements of each model but does not attempt a complete description of each.

One of the earliest models was developed by Carkhuff (1969). The model employs a two-phase format through which the trainee develops skills to cover the seven dimensions of the counselor role (Delworth and Aulepp, 1976). In the first phase the student develops facilitative or responsive skills, and in the second phase the student develops action-oriented or initiative skills (Meade, 1978). This training often has been called "empathy training," since empathy is the most important skill that trainees develop. This particular approach does not require extensive equipment. Tape recorders can be used to develop responding skills, but they are not essential.

A second model was developed by Ivey (1971). Called microcounseling, it involves videotape demonstrations of specific skills and the practice of those skills on a skill-by-skill basis. By practicing each skill separately, the trainees have a chance to develop each skill independently of the others, and the videotaping allows them to critique their individual performances. An obvious drawback to this approach is that it requires expensive videotape equipment. Without it, this approach to helping skills should not be considered.

Another approach that uses tapes, as well as films and printed material, is Interpersonal Process Recall (Kagan, 1975). This method uses videotapes to focus on all the dynamics of the interview situation. Unlike microcounseling, it does not examine specific skills. Kagan has developed a series of developmental tasks that form the basis for the training, but it is the recall aspect of the interview that really is the heart of the model. This model requires the same equipment as microcounseling—videotape, cameras, and monitors. Moreover, the approach requires a very skilled trainer. Such a degree of training is not usual in people who typically conduct RA training: entry-level residence hall directors.

Egan (1975) developed an approach that does not require any special equipment. This method uses a book and a workbook of exercises to train individuals along seven counselor dimensions. To develop helping skills, the workbook provides sequential practice for each of the counselor dimensions.

This approach is easily adapted to the training of residence life staff. However, some of the exercises in the workbook are difficult for college-age trainees, since the role plays involve situations—a dying woman as client and minister as counselor—that are somewhat foreign to college students.

Another model was developed by Danish and Hauer (1973). This model is very tightly organized and provides a systematic approach to the development of helping skills (Meade, 1978). Since the approach is so systematic, it can be especially useful for residence life staff who have a strong need for structure. It does not require special equipment.

It should be clear that there is no best model to employ. As Meade (1978) points out, there is no definitive research that singles out one best approach. The individual exigencies of any campus will determine the most desirable model for training resident assistants. It is clear, however, that the best results attend a systematic approach.

There are a number of resource people who might be called on to assist in this type of training. Individuals in the student counseling center come most quickly to mind; their experience and training make them invaluable teachers of helping skills. Additionally, graduate students in counselor education, psychology, or sociology might be employed on a practicum basis to assist in training residence life staff in helping skills. Also, allied professionals, such as campus ministers, would be excellent for this type of training. Many ministers have graduate training in guidance and counseling. They could share this knowledge with residence life staff who need helping skills.

There are a number of other human relations skills upon which to base staff training. These skills relate to providing services to special constituencies. Although not all these skills are appropriate for all institutions of higher education, some skills of value with special constituencies are very appropriate. Special helping skills in alcohol awareness and abuse, depression and suicide prevention, anti-racism training, assertiveness training, human sexuality, gay awareness, rape awareness, drug and substance use and abuse, and anti-sexism or personal liberation would be welcome on many campuses. Training in these areas can be through films, videotapes, audiotapes, and paper-and-pencil exercises. Specific training programs can be tailored to meet individual campus needs. In summary, it is critical to help resident assistants develop skills in effective interaction. If staff are ineffective in dealing with people, they will be unsuccessful in their positions. The most successful training is systematic and uses a comprehensive plan to build skills onto skills. Such an approach fosters improved human relations skills in staff—skills they will need to deal with people, especially students, on a daily basis.

Training in Programming/Advising

There appears to be considerable agreement in student development literature (Brown, 1972; Chickering, 1974; Coons, 1974; and Miller and Prince, 1976) that college students undergo certain developmental changes while they are enrolled in institutions of higher education. Obviously, this development varies widely from student to student, but there appears to be substantial concurrence that students develop in a variety of ways. Moreover, research findings (Astin, 1977; Chickering, 1974) support the concept that students who live in residence halls develop faster than those who live off campus. Chickering (1974a), in particular, builds a strong case for the positive educational impact of residence hall life on students. These conclusions underscore the importance of resident assistants who are trained in programming and advising skills and can provide leadership in program development in residence halls.

Student staff often will find themselves in roles as planners of programs or advisers to students planning programs. Systematic, thorough program planning is essential but student needs assessment should precede program planning. Aulepp and Delworth (1976) and Huebner (1979) provide detailed methods of assessing and designing campus environments. These authors give much useful information, but by and large their approaches are too sophisticated for resident assistants. However, there are other methods by which student staff can assess the needs and interests of residents.

One method is interest matching (Schuh, 1978). In this method RAs ask students at an initial floor meeting to indicate their special interests on an index card and to list on the same card skills they would be willing to teach others. In a short period of time the resident assistant has sufficient data to match students by interests, introduce them to each other, and develop seminars and instruction in activities, sports, handicrafts, and so on. Another approach to developing a data bank of student interests is the student interest survey. This approach is somewhat more sophisticated. Each student receives a detailed list of activities and checks off activities of interest. The object is to match students who have similar interests. Of course matching student interests is most useful in program planning early in the academic year.

There are many ways to go about training staff in program planning. One source for such information is a monograph edited by Schuh (1977) that presents a number of approaches to developing specialized programs and provides an overview to programming skills. One effective means of developing programming capability in staff is to use a checklist of activities that need to be completed before a program can be scheduled. After they receive the checklist staff are asked to plan a program during the first week the residence halls are open. The activity need not be terribly complex; it could be as simple as an ice cream social or a softball game with another hall. When the program is over, the staff should be assembled for debriefing. At this session the residence hall director elicits and answers questions. If the staff's first programming experience is positive, they will be much more likely to undertake other programming efforts. Thus, this first program should be simple and easy to plan. The RA's supervisor should be especially liberal with support and guidance during the planning of this first program.

Much of the programming that will take place in the resident assistant's unit, however, will be planned by students themselves. In this case the resident assistant assumes a different role—group adviser. This role calls for a number of special skills. Fortunately, there are a number of resources useful in developing these skills in the resident assistant. Bloland's (1967) standard work on this form of advising details the role of the group adviser. Bloland's work can be adapted into handouts for resident assistants. The National Orientation Directors Association's handbook (Van Hecke, 1978) has an excellent chapter on program planning and useful information on funding and budgeting for student activities. The chapter on fiscal management is particularly appropriate for resident assistants advising student groups with a budget. Technical Appendix B of Moore and Delworth's (1976) monograph on student service program development is quite useful in describing group roles. Highly recommended, it provides a solid basis for training staff in group process skills. Training staff to assume an advisory role is much like training staff in programming roles: careful supervision to correct initial errors benefits both advisers and advisees.

One last aspect of programmatic training is evaluation. There are two aspects to this training. One is to help staff develop a philosophical basis for evaluation; the other is to ensure that some form of evaluation is conducted in all programs. The philosophical question can be a difficult one, since many staff assume the successful program is the well-attended one. This assumption is dangerous, since some programs—such as highly-specialized handicraft programs—are not meant to be heavily attended. Moreover, if staff evaluate strictly on participation they may believe a well-attended program has been successful even though that program failed to meet the participants' expectations. Thus, the best philosophical approach to evaluation may be to ask this simple question: Were the expectations of the participants met by the program? To address the second aspect, the simplest way to ensure that an evaluation is conducted for all events is to build that requirement into the planning process. Evaluation should appear on the planning checklist, and an evaluation report should be routinely filed with all program summaries.

The emphasis on programmatic development in residence halls has increased significantly over the past decade. Students expect and often demand a series of good programs in their residential centers. Because of student expectations and because of the profession's commitment to enriching the lives of students, it is imperative that residence hall staff develop programming and advising skills. Development of these skills can only enhance the success of a residence hall operation.

Other Training Issues

Team building and developing staff unity are vital aspects of training. Team building is often perceived as a by-product of other training activities and therefore is not addressed as a separate training issue. That is a mistake. In fact, if team building is addressed early and often in the training process, other training components will be facilitated. That is, staff will be more receptive to other training after they have grown to accept and trust their fellow staff members as working colleagues. For this reason, some attention needs to be given to developing a staff team. There are many good exercises (Jones and Pfeiffer, 1979) that can be used for this purpose. The exercises are simple, yet they do an excellent job of developing a staff team.

One other note about team building and morale: It is very helpful if each hall has a committee whose purpose is to promote staff morale. Residence hall staffs suffer from mental and physical exhaustion at certain strategic points in the academic year; this committee should plan activities that will boost sagging morale. Remembering birthdays, celebrating special holidays, planning excursions, and so on all are functions of the morale committee. Their work will do much to preserve the cohesion and good spirits of a heavily taxed staff.

The preparation and use of the staff manual has been discussed briefly in conjunction with some training activities mentioned earlier. Often the manual is a long, cumbersome document that is overwhelming to new staff members. There are several guidelines to use in the preparing this document. First, include in the manual only these items that you expect staff to use. There is no point in impressing your supervisors with the thickness of your manual if staff will not use these materials. Second, make the material easy to read and remember. If appropriate, devote a separate page to each policy or procedure that you expect staff to master or devote one page to each outside service. Keep the format simple. Third, think of the manual as a working document that must reflect changes in services and procedures. A ringbinder with loose-leaf sheets might be much more effective than a bound document. Fourth, if you are serious about having staff master the material in the manual, devote training time to it. Simply distributing the manual and expecting staff to read it in their spare time will not suffice. Refer to Rickgarn (1978) for a more complete discussion of staff manuals.

One last training method that deserves mention is the use of case studies. Case studies provide vivid descriptions of situations that are useful in staff training. They are most effective if they reflect real situations encountered in the residence halls. Chamberlain and Werner (1980) developed an excellent set of case studies that give good training results.

Staffs that are particularly large — over one hundred — or very small — under ten — pose special problems. Staffs that range between ten and one hundred can be trained on both centralized and decentralized bases. The numbers allow for workable centralized training classes. Staffs much larger than one hundred require decentralized training, much of it in individual residential areas. This approach requires training skills on the part of hall directors; central residence life staff then assume advisory roles. For example, it is more difficult to arrange for a number of sessions led by a department head than to arrange for one mass meeting. This situation is typical of the planning and logistical problems that come with particularly large staffs. Similarly, very small staffs can pose problems. Very small groups are unlikely to draw much central support, and their trainers must be inventive, self-reliant, and knowledgeable since they can expect little outside assistance. The special problems posed by very large or very small staffs are not insurmountable, but they need to be recognized and confronted.

Summary

This chapter has three purposes: The first is to suggest some general areas in which to train resident assistants. These areas include operational services, institutional support services, human relations skills, and programming/advising skills. A good training program addresses each of these areas. The second purpose is to present various training options. Trainers should choose options appropriate to their needs. The third issue is developing a structure for staff training programs. The sequence of training and the role of the staff manual must be considered. A recurring point is that training must be sequential: skills are built onto skills, and logic of succession must inform all training.

There is no foolproof blueprint for success in developing a staff training program. However, several keys to success are assessing the training needs of the staff, knowing what training resources are available, sequencing the training, and being flexible enough to make necessary changes in the training program. Success is likely if one keeps these keys in mind, disregarding them means almost certain failure.

References

Astin, A. W. *Four Critical Years: Effects of College on Beliefs, Attitudes, and Knowledge*. San Francisco: Jossey-Bass, 1977.

Aulepp, L., and Delworth, U. *Training Manual for an Ecosystem Model: Assessing and Designing Campus Environment*. Boulder, Colo.: Western Interstate Commission for Higher Education, 1976.

Bloland, P. *Student Group Advising in Higher Education*. Student Personnel Series, No. 8. Washington, D.C.: American College Personnel Association, 1967.

Brown, R. D. *Student Development in Tomorrow's Higher Education — A Return to the Academy*. Student Personnel Series, No. 16. Washington, D.C.: American College Personnel Association, 1972.

Carkhuff, R. R. *Helping and Human Relations*. Vols. 1 and 2. New York: Holt, Rinehart and Winston, 1969.

Chamberlain, P. C., and Werner, W. L. *A Problem Solving Casebook for Residence Hall Administrators*. Bloomington, Ind.: Association of College and University Housing Officers, 1980.

Chickering, A. W. *Commuting Versus Resident Students: Overcoming Educational Inequities of Living Off Campus*. San Francisco: Jossey-Bass, 1974.

Chickering, A. W. "Education and Identity: Implications for Residence Hall Living." In D. DeCoster and P. Mable (Eds.), *Student Development and Education In College Residence Halls*. Cincinnati, Ohio: American College Personnel Association, 1974a.

Coons, F. "The Developmental Tasks of College Students." In D. DeCoster and P. Mable (Eds.), *Student Development and Education in College Residence Halls*. Cincinnati, Ohio: American College Personnel Association, 1974.

Danish, S. J., and Hauer, A. L. *Helping Skills: A Basic Training Program.* New York: Behavioral Publications, 1973.

DeCoster, D., and Mable, P. "Residence Education: Purpose and Process." In D. DeCoster and P. Mable (Eds.), *Student Development and Education in College Residence Halls.* Cincinnati, Ohio: American College Personnel Association, 1974.

Delworth, U. (Ed.). *New Directions for Student Services: Training Competent Staff,* no. 2. San Francisco: Jossey-Bass, 1978.

Delworth, U., and Aulepp, L. *Training Manual for Paraprofessional and Allied Professional Programs.* Boulder, Colo.: Western Interstate Commission for Higher Education, 1976.

Delworth, U., and Yarris, E. "Concepts and Processes for the New Training Role." In U. Delworth (Ed.), *New Directions for Student Services: Training Competent Staff,* no. 2. San Francisco: Jossey-Bass, 1978.

Egan, G. *The Skilled Helper: A Model for Systematic Helping and Interpersonal Relating.* Monterey, Calif.: Brooks/Cole, 1975.

Huebner, L. (Ed.). *New Directions for Student Services: Redesigning Campus Environments,* no. 8. San Francisco: Jossey-Bass, 1979.

Ivey, A. E. *Microcounseling: Innovations in Interviewer Training.* Springfield, Ill.: Thomas, 1971.

Jones, J. E., and Pfeiffer, J. U. (Eds.). *The 1979 Annual Handbook for Group Facilitators.* La Jolla, Calif.: University Associates, 1979.

Kagan, N. *Interpersonal Process Recall: A Method of Influencing Human Interaction.* East Lansing: Michigan State University, Educational Publication Services, 1975.

Meade, C. J. "Interpersonal Skills: Who, What, When, Why." In U. Delworth (Ed.), *New Directions for Student Services: Training Competent Staff,* no. 2. San Francisco: Jossey-Bass, 1978.

Miller, T. K., and Prince, J. S. *The Future of Student Affairs: A Guide to Student Development for Tomorrow's Higher Education.* San Francisco: Jossey-Bass, 1976.

Moore, M., and Delworth, U. *Training Manual for Student Service Program Development.* Boulder, Colo.: Western Interstate Commission for Higher Education, 1976.

Powell, J. R. "Inservice Education for Student Staff." In D. DeCoster and P. Mable (Eds.), *Student Development and Education in College Residence Halls.* Cincinnati, Ohio: American College Personnel Association, 1974.

Rickgarn, R. L. "Manuals: Their Development and Use in Training." In U. Delworth (Ed.), *New Directions for Student Services: Training Competent Staff,* no. 2. San Francisco: Jossey-Bass, 1978.

Schuh, J. H. (Ed.). *Programming and Activities in College and University Residence Halls.* Bloomington, Ind.: Association of College and University Housing Officers, 1977.

Schuh, J. H. "An Easy Student Interest Assessment." *Journal of College Student Personnel,* 1978, *19*(3), 475.

Shelton, J. L., and Corazzini, J. G. "The Referral Process in the College Community: Some Guidelines for Residence Hall Paraprofessionals." *Journal of the National Association of Women Deans, Administrators and Counselors,* Spring 1976, *39*(3), 102–106.

Van Hecke, C. E. (Ed.). *Handbook for Orientation Directors.* National Orientation Directors Association, 1978.

*John H. Schuh is director of the Department of Residence Life and
part-time associate professor of college student personnel administration
at Indiana University, Bloomington. He is a former assistant
director of housing and adjunct professor of education at Arizona
State University. He is a member of the Executive Committee of the
Association of College and University Housing Officers.*

*This chapter looks forward to the future of residence halls,
predicts major influences and their effects, and tells how to
prepare for what is to come.*

Influences, Predictions, and Recommendations

Gregory S. Blimling
John H. Schuh

Predicting the future is a little like hitting balloons on a carnival dart board.
Some balloons are easier to hit than others, but the darts are weighted against
you. At best, predicting the future is a risky venture. Nonetheless, this chapter
will attempt to identify the major influences on higher education, speculate on
the effects these influences will have on residence halls, and make some recommendations for preparing for the future.

Major Influences

Enrollment. There is no question that enrollment will decline in the
next decade. That trend is assured by demographic statistics reflecting the
declining birth rate. The Carnegie Council on Policy Studies in Higher Education (1980) estimates that the decline in college-age people (eighteen to
twenty-four years old) will be 23 percent by 1997. The decline will come in
stages: enrollments will remain relatively stable until 1983 and then decline
until about 1988. For the next two years after that enrollment will remain con-
stant and decline sharply between 1991 and 1997. The Midwest and the East
will be hardest hit by these declines, losing as much as ten percent of their current share of the college population. As the population of the nation continues

to move into the sunbelt states, colleges in the South, Southwest, and West will gain between five and ten percent of the total college population (Carnegie Council on Policy Studies in Higher Education, 1980). Prestigious Ivy League colleges and major state universities will not be affected as much by enrollment declines as less selective private institutions, two-year colleges, and state colleges far from urban centers. Though some of these declines will be offset by increased enrollment of part-time and older students, it is unlikely that these students will be interested in living in college residence halls as they now exist.

We will continue to compete for those traditional college students, with the lure of off-campus housing forcing us into either marketing the advantages of residence halls or retreating to establishing parietal regulations requiring students to live in residence halls. In either case, we must be prepared to offer sound educational reasons for the benefits of the residential experience to the students as consumers or to the courts as guardians of students' rights.

Economic Influences. Any person who has worked in higher education for the past decade can expound on the deleterious effects of inflation on the cost of everything from fuel to computer paper. Inflation hurts everyone and every institution — but not equally. Labor-intensive institutions, such as universities, suffer more because they are less able to pass along increased costs to the consumer (through tuition increases) (Murphy, 1980). This has been evident at several universities, but not so graphically as at the City University of New York, which raised tuition and experienced a staggering enrollment decline that sent the university into a major financial slump (Simon, 1980).

Inflation is a multidimensional problem for higher education. It affects universities directly through rising costs, indirectly through the diminishing ability of people to afford a college education, and subjectively through the lost faith of the public in the ability of higher education to provide economic rewards. This loss in faith has been a recent phenomenon. For years higher education was offered to the American public as the way to greater financial rewards: few admissions counselors could not recite dollar differences in lifetime salaries of college graduates (compared to high school graduates). This motivation for attending college faded a few years ago when the economy sagged and universities graduated their largest senior classes ever. As tales of Ph.D. graduates working as postal clerks were reported by the media and the starting salaries of college professors were compared with the wages of apprentice plumbers and San Francisco sanitation workers, the public lost confidence in the ability of higher education to provide the "good life" as defined by monetary rewards.

Thus inability of universities to pass on inflationary costs, negative effects of inflation on people's ability to afford college, and weakened confidence in the financial advantages of a college education pose a financial dilemma for higher education in the coming decade. Add increasing demands for educational services, declining high school populations, enrollment-based formulas for state funding of public higher education, and less federal support for research and the financial picture for higher education looks rather bleak.

Consumerism, retention, and *retrenchment* will be the key words in the coming decade of fiscal frugality. What characteristics will attract students to an institution? How can students be retained at the institution? What programs and services, not central to the mission of the institution, can be eliminated? These will be the significant questions raised during the coming decade.

As auxiliary budget items under bonded indebtedness, residence halls at most institutions may have some insulation against the most overt retrenchment. At the same time, residence halls are most susceptible to the effects of rising energy costs and declining enrollment. From a purely economic standpoint (although students who wish to live off campus will argue this point) room and board in a residence hall are less expensive than most off-campus housing. Keeping the room and board rate low is contingent on high occupancy; and high occupancy, since fewer students will enter the residence halls, will depend on high retention. In turn, retention is related to responding to the needs of students, or consumerism.

Student Characteristics. Since World War II the population of students attending institutions of higher education has become more heterogeneous, and if declining SAT and ACT scores are to be believed, less prepared for college work. The American Council on Education (1980) suggests further diversification of students as a way of offsetting declining enrollments. Their suggestions to increase the number of eighteen- to twenty-four-year-old students include: (1) increasing the number of foreign students, (2) increasing the enrollment of young people from lower- and middle-income groups, (3) increasing the percentage of high school dropouts who take the high school equivalence test, (4) increasing the number of minority high school graduates, and (5) increasing the overall percentage of students graduating from high school. As these students enter colleges, they will bring with them values, behaviors, and cultural qualities unique to their backgrounds and experiences. Many of these new students will have special needs; they will require special assistance adjusting to the college environment. Much of this adjustment will take place in the residence halls.

Government Regulations. There is no reason to believe that the increased governmental regulations of higher education in the past decade will decrease in the next. Legislative acts—Section 504 of the Rehabilitation Act of 1973, which called for facilities changes on most campuses; the Family Educational Rights and Privacy Act of 1974, which in some cases caused universities to set rather elaborate guidelines for the use and release of information; and the application of the Fair Labor Standards Act of 1963 to resident assistants and residence hall professional staff, which caused residence hall administrators to evaluate job descriptions in light of minimum wage guidelines—will continue to utilize the time and resources of universities.

Reflecting legislative trends, the courts are likely to continue viewing the student-institutional relationship as one of consumer to commodity provider. They will continue to expect universities to abandon "in loco parentis" control yet retain responsibility for the physical security of students.

Predictions

From this analysis emerge the following predictions about residence halls in the coming decade:
1. Enrollment declines due to fewer high school students and economic constraints will mean lower occupancy for residence halls on many campuses.
2. Inflation, enrollment declines, and related economic factors will force universities into retrenchment, open admissions, and concentration upon retention.
3. Since they will be able to choose more freely among universities, students as consumers will demand more services, better facilities, and more freedom in residence halls.
4. Universities will be asked to meet the needs of a more diversified student population.
5. The government will continue to regulate universities, and more university policies and actions will be challenged in the courts.

Analysis and Recommendations

Residence hall administrators cannot escape these influences, but they can minimize their negative implications by preparing for inevitable changes.

Facilities. The most obvious approach to lessening the effects of decreased occupancy is to modify facilities to accommodate a variety of functions. Some possible adaptations are abandoning standard double occupancy rooms in favor of apartment-type suites, renting halls for conference suites, renting halls for conference housing, and converting entire buildings into low-cost housing for the elderly or the disadvantaged. Moreover, some buildings could be used for handicapped children or for children who require similar custodial care and cannot live with their parents. On campuses where there is a shortage of academic space and an overabundance of student living space, converting residence halls to offices is an obvious solution.

Students have a great concern for privacy. Many are asking for unshared living quarters and less regular interaction with others. Colleges can capitalize on this trend by giving students the option of living alone in two-person rooms in exchange for a higher room rent. This practice is already common on many campuses at the middle of the academic year; if occupancy falls it can be done the year round. Many students would welcome this option, which might be especially attractive to upperclass students, older students, or those who simply desire more privacy.

Decreased demand for student housing will mean vigorous marketing to attract prospective residents. Universities cannot otherwise hope to fill residence halls. In the past institutions have done nothing more than fill orders for rooms. That approach will need to change if there is to be any hope of high occupancy.

Staff. While it is obvious that facilities will need to undergo certain changes in the future, the future of residence life staff is less clear. Changes will be necessary, but the direction of these changes is still somewhat difficult to determine. Several possibilities exist.

One possibility is greater reliance on student staff. A number of institutions already utilize undergraduate students instead of full-time professionals as hall directors. One would think that this approach would yield fewer services for students, but the converse is true in that students must assume a much larger role in planning and decision-making and in the day-to-day operation of the hall.

Another possibility is to utilize professional staff on a part-time basis in the residence halls and fill the balance of their time with collateral assignments in student affairs, business affairs, or some other aspect of campus administration. This approach has been successfully adopted at a number of institutions where staff spend half the day in the residence center and the balance of their time in judicial affairs, student activities, or some other phase of student development services. Part-time use of faculty to run residence halls may be another solution to the staffing problems of the future. Perhaps a return to the concept of Oxford and Cambridge would be a positive step in meeting the financial challenges of the future.

To meet the student needs identified by the American Council on Education (1980), to assist students in adjusting to college, and to promote a positive exchange of values and culture within the residence hall, professional and undergraduate staff will need strong human relations skills, as Ostroth points out in the sixth chapter. They must also undergo intensive, systematic training, as Schuh outlines in the seventh chapter.

Student personnel preparation programs will need to be more versatile than they are now. To prepare prospective professionals for positions in student housing alone may be too narrow an approach. Student personnel professionals will need more exposure to business and academic affairs.

Research. Residential administrators will need to assert the importance of the residential educational experience to colleagues in the university and to the general public. Research studies clearly underscore the benefits of the residential experience. Though these findings have been available for several years, residential educators have not been active in sharing the information with academic and administrative colleagues, students, and the general public. Moreover, research should be conducted to substantiate national findings in local settings. Examples of local research projects include environmental assessment evaluations, comparative studies of predicted and earned grade point averages, retention studies, and student satisfaction projects, all of which should provide a data base for the impact of residential programs on students. Faculty involvement in these projects is important and easily secured.

Faculty participation as coresearchers or consultants will give credibility to the various research and evaluation projects. The projects, in turn, will help provide a definitive profile of residential life on campus.

Educational Programs. Schroeder's and Rowe's chapters tell us that student retention can be increased by permitting students greater control over their environments and by structuring the peer environment through living and learning centers to engage students in the process of their own learning. By linking living and learning centers to academic programs, as Rowe suggests; by focusing on developmental programming, as Leafgren recommends; and by having universities adopt outcomes for students that include affective development, as Blimling suggests, education in the residence halls will not only promote the retention of students but also align itself with the central academic mission of universities.

In the next decade programs will need to be designed to meet the varying academic needs of the student community. Much of the programmatic emphasis in the past has been upon social and recreational programming, and not enough attention has been devoted to academic and academic-support programs. We need a new approach: programs in residence halls will have to provide a learning component that is as important to students as classroom learning.

Student participation in the operation and development of the residence hall program will have increased importance in the future. A broader variety of housing options—to include intentional democratic communities, cooperatives, and other independent units—will need to be developed to meet the needs of a broader variety of students. Specialized housing for older students also will need to be planned, and greater emphasis must be placed on the role of the student in hall governance, including student involvement in policy development, program planning, and fiscal management. Students expect such involvement, and their contributions from their perspective as consumers are crucial.

Another way to adapt the residence hall to the future is to cater to special groups of students. Students studying a foreign language, students sharing a special interest and students with the same academic major might share housing. Other groupings are twenty-four quiet units, honors units, or units developed on the basis of unique career expectations of the residents. Although the future may not be bright, it offers opportunities to explore new specialized options for housing and broadens our choices. We can no longer assume, as Leafgren points out in the third chapter, that the educational benefits of residence hall living will materialize merely by talking about them, or that students will absorb the educational experience of residence halls by staying around them long enough. Leaving the personal development of students to chance is not enough. If we fail to achieve a meaningful educational experience in the residence halls, we will move down a path leading to a managerial custodianship of buildings.

Recommendations

1. The educational development of the student through the residence halls must become central to the mission of the university by (a) having the concept of the educated person adopted as the principal mission of the university, (b) developing living and learning centers and similar programs in conjunction with academic programs, (c) adopting a developmental philosophy toward students and toward the design of educational programs for the residence halls, and (d) working as a team both with student personnel professionals in other departments and with academic and administrative departments.

2. Residence hall administrators must focus upon retention to provide stable occupancy and low-cost room and board. This can be accomplished through increasing student control over their living environments, structuring the peer environment to increase the community experience in residence halls, and providing developmental programs in the residence halls.

3. Facilities will need to be redesigned to accommodate many functions: suites for students, conference facilities, and perhaps cooperative housing for students and the elderly or other special groups.

4. A systematic approach to the selection and training of undergraduate resident assistants will need to be undertaken to compensate for cutbacks in professional staff and increased needs on the part of students who may be ill-prepared for college life.

5. Professional staff members will need broader graduate training to assume multiple roles in the educational development of students.

Taken together, these recommendations have the goal of placing student housing within the academic mainstream of campus life and removing it from a peripheral or auxiliary role. There is no question that when student residential programs achieve that goal, they will make a significant contribution to the recruitment and retention of students and boost the vitality of the institution. Should residential programs not be viewed in that way, they will be earmarked for budget reductions or elimination altogether.

There are no simple solutions to the future problems of college residence halls. Creative approaches in marrying the academic program with residential life will solve many potential problems. If such planning has not been undertaken, colleges and universities would be well advised to begin immediate preparations for the next decade. Their survival may depend on it.

References

American Council on Education. *Educational Enrollment: Testing the Conventional Wisdom Against the Facts.* Washington, D.C.: American Council on Education, 1980.

Carnegie Council on Policy Studies in Higher Education. *Three Thousand Futures: The Next Twenty Years for Higher Education.* San Francisco: Jossey-Bass, 1980.

Murphy, F. "The University and the Perilous Eighties." *Vital Speeches of the Day,* Feb. 15, 1980, *46* (9), 279–281.

Simon, P. "The Changing Economy and Its Effects on Services, Professionals, and Students: A Cautionary Note." In D. Creamer (Ed.), *Student Development in Higher Education.* Cincinnati, Ohio: American College Personnel Association, 1980.

Gregory S. Blimling is associate dean of students at Louisiana State University, Baton Rouge.

John H. Schuh is director, department of Residence Life at Indiana University, Bloomington.

These concise descriptions of recommended literature acquaint residence education professionals with work in the field.

Annotated References

Janice L. Diehl

The annotated references list new sources of information about residence halls or highlight sources that have not been given the exposure they deserve. Books and articles that might be considered standard works in student personnel and residence life are not reviewed.

Aulepp, L., and Delworth, U. *Training Manual for an Ecosystem Model: Assessing and Designing Campus Environments.* Boulder, Colo.: Western Interstate Commission for Higher Education, 1976.

    This publication provides a detailed guide for implementing the ecosystem model in redesigning campus environments. The five major stages of the procedure are discussed; specific techniques and assessment instruments are described.

Bellucci, J. E. "Affective Simulation in a Resident Assistant Training Program." *Journal of the National Association for Women Deans, Administrators, and Counselors,* 1976, *36*(3), 107–111.

    Kagan's interpersonal process recall (IPR) stimulus films were used in a helping skills training program for resident assistants. The author proposes these films as a potential screening device for staff selection.

Blimling, G., and Milterberger, L. *The Resident Assistant: Working with College Students in Residence Halls.* Dubuque, Iowa: Kendall/Hunt Publishing, 1981.

Written as a textbook for use in undergraduate resident assistant training programs, this book focuses on the educational role of the resident assistant in the development of students. The book is written as a practical skill-building text on contemporary issues confronting resident assistants.

Buckner, D. R. "Restructuring Residence Hall Programming: Residence Hall Educators with a Curriculum." *Journal of College Student Personnel,* 1977, *18*(5), 389–392.

Buckner relates the development and resulting difficulties of residence hall programming as it has traditionally been accomplished in American colleges and universities. A rationale is developed for a revised staffing pattern and a different approach to programming. The implementation of one such restructuring at Northern Illinois University is described.

Corazzini, J. G., and Wilson, S. "Students, the Environment, and Their Interaction: Assessing Student Needs and Planning for Change." *Journal of the National Association for Women Deans, Administrators, and Counselors,* 1977, *40*(2), 68–72.

The authors propose modifying the environment rather than counseling the individual as an alternative in helping students meet their needs. The introduction provides a sound rationale for the application of such intentional campus design interventions. A case study of one attempt at Colorado State University is presented. The difficulties encountered are explored, and recommendations for future environmental interventions are offered.

Creamer, D. (Ed.). *Student Development in Higher Education: Theories, Practices, and Future Directions.* Washington, D.C.: American College Personnel Association, 1980.

This book presents the basic concepts and conceptual components of student development in higher education. Organized into fifteen chapters, it is divided into four major units as follows: "Theories, Concepts and Ethics"; "Environmental Considerations"; "Practices and Future Directions"; and "Barriers." Each chapter focuses on one issue central to the implementation of student development within higher education.

DeCoster, D. A., and Mable, P. (Eds.). *Student Development and Education in College Residence Halls.* Cincinnati, Ohio: American College Personnel Association, 1974.

This book is a resource for student development specialists particularly interested in residence education. Its chapters are adaptations of workshop presentations sponsored by Commission III of the American College Personnel Association. The philosophical foundations of residence education are discussed. The impact of residence life personnel and the environment on student development are considered.

DeCoster, D. A., and Mable, P. (Eds.). *Personal Education and Community Development in College Residence Halls.* Cincinnati, Ohio: American College Personnel Association, 1980.

The nineteen chapters of this book are organized into four major sections as follows: "Personal Development and Education"; "Human Relationships and Community Development"; "The Developmental Process: Educators and Students"; and "Knowing the Past, Planning the Future." Focusing upon student development in residence halls, the book examines the role of educators in helping students assess and realize their personal objectives through developmental programs and systematic evaluation.

Delworth, U. (Ed.). *New Directions for Student Services: Training Competent Staff,* no. 2. San Francisco: Jossey-Bass, 1978.

Contributors present information to assist student affairs professionals in their roles as developers, implementers, and evaluators of pre- and in-service training programs for both professional and paraprofessional staff members. Knowledge needed to organize effective programs is discussed, as are various training models and specific innovative training techniques. Suggestions for quality supervision and evaluation of staff development programs are included.

Delworth, U., and Aulepp, L. *Training Manual for Paraprofessional and Allied Professional Programs.* Boulder, Colo.: Western Interstate Commission for Higher Education, 1976.

The authors provide supplemental information for planning student service programs to be used in conjunction with the model presented in Moore and Delworth (1976), cited below. They address the issue of the involvement and training of student volunteers, paraprofessionals, and allied professionals in student development programs.

Ender, K., Kane, N., Mable, P., and Strohm, M. *Creating Community in Residence Design and Delivery.* Cincinnati, Ohio: American College Personnel Association, 1980.

This thirty-page workbook is designed for individual students or small student groups. It guides the student through defining *community,* designing a community, and the implementing a community within the residence halls.

Flanagan, D. *The Effects of College and University Residential Program on Students.* (ERIC Document Reproduction Service No. ED 111 252)

Flanagan identifies those elements of college residential living that have proved beneficial in creating meaningful experiences for students, summarizes the conclusions educators have drawn from previous research regarding difficulties of residential living, and attempts to combine this information into proposals for effective living learning programs.

Frichette, S. R. "Cooperative Housing for Students." *The Journal of College and University Student Housing,* 1972, *2* (1), 30–34.

The purpose of this study was to determine the number and kinds of cooperative housing units in colleges and universities across the United States. The term *cooperative housing unit* is defined, and a brief history of the development of such units is included.

German, S. C. "Selecting Undergraduate Paraprofessionals on College Campuses: A Review." *Journal of College Student Personnel, 1979, 20* (1), 28–34.

This investigator reviews the literature regarding variables, instruments, and procedures for selecting student paraprofessional counselors in postsecondary institutions. The author gives summaries and evaluations of various procedures and considers implications and recommendations for selections and future research. While German focuses exclusively on counseling, which is only one of the many responsibilities of the resident assistant, this article is directly applicable to selection of any type of campus paraprofessional.

Greenwood, J. D., and Lembcke, B. (Eds.). *Student Staff in College Residence Halls: Educational Preparation and Role Clarification.* Cincinnati, Ohio: American College Personnel Association, 1975.

This book reports results of research conducted by Commission III of the American College Personnel Association on residence hall student staff role definitions and training. Several training programs are analyzed, key issues are investigated, and recommendations for improvement are offered.

Hammond, E. H., and Shaffer, R. H. *The Legal Foundations of Student Personnel Services in Higher Education.* American College Personnel Association monograph. Washington, D.C.: American College Personnel and Guidance Association, 1978.

The purpose of this monograph is to alert the student personnel professional to legal developments and issues that apply to student development work in higher education. Several authors discuss specific legislation that has critical and direct implications for student personnel services; others approach the issue by focusing on actual operations in student affairs and then illustrating the law's influence therein. An entire chapter is devoted to the subject of staff liability. The final chapter offers projections of future legal concerns and potential developments in the student affairs field. Legal issues and cases directly applied to residential living are presented and discussed. References and a bibliography are included.

Magnarella, P. J. "The Continuing Evaluation of a Living Learning Center." *Journal of College Student Personnel,* 1979, *20* (1), 4–9.

This article describes and evaluates a two-year-old living learning center (LLC) at the University of Vermont. It compares participants' perceptions of the LLC and its program with their views of previous experiences in traditional residence centers.

Moore, M., and Delworth, U. *Training Manual for Student Service Program Development.* Boulder, Colo.: Western Interstate Commission for Higher Education, 1976.

Moore and Delworth describe a five-stage model of a systematic approach for the design and implementation of student development programs. The model derives from the cube model (Morrill, W. H., Oetting, E. R., and Hurst, J. C. "Dimensions of Counselor Functioning." *Personnel and Guidance Journal,* 1974, *54,* 355-369) and is an expansion of earlier work by the authors.

Moos, R. H. "Social Environments of University Student Living Groups: Architectural and Organizational Correlates." *Environment and Behavior,* March 1978, *10,* 109-126.

Moos employed a sample of eighty-seven student living groups from sixteen diverse college and university campuses across the United States to investigate the relationships among physical design, organizational structure and function and psychosocial characteristics and climate. The results indicate that the percentage of single rooms and the location of the living unit on campus were the two most influential physical-architectural characteristics, whereas the most potent organizational characteristics involved programming, especially the number of guest lectures and intramural activities. The author proposes that the social environment of a living group may diminish the impact of architectural and organizational characteristics and concludes with a discussion of the special usefulness of different evaluation methods of student living environments.

O'Donnell, W. J., and Oglesby, C. L. "Paraprofessional Counselor Training for Residence Hall Personnel." *The Journal of College and University Student Housing,* 1978-1979, *8* (2), 25-26.

Counseling techniques that help students understand and solve problems are combined into a five-lesson package for the training of residence hall personnel in paraprofessional counseling skills. The roles of the participants and instructor(s) are outlined. Suggestions for increased effectiveness are included.

Parker, C. (Ed.). *Encouraging Development in College Students.* Minneapolis: University of Minnesota Press, 1978.

This twelve-chapter book leads the reader through a clarification of much recent human relations and stage development theory to a sound examination of the influence college has upon the development of students. It is a clear statement of how students develop in college and how student development educators help students fulfill their goals.

Schroeder, C. C. "Territoriality: Conceptual and Methodological Issues for Residence Educators." *The Journal of College and University Student Housing,* 1978-1979, *8* (2), 9-15.

Schroeder proposes that despite the potentially constructive influence of territoriality on student development and satisfaction, residence educators have virtually ignored the relationship between student behavior and the physical environment. In this article the author explains the concept of territoriality, describes its effects, and discusses strategies by residence educators to facilitate student growth.

Schroeder, C. C., Anchors, S., and Jackson, S. *Making Yourself at Home.* Cincinnati, Ohio: American College Personnel Association, 1978.

The authors discuss the concepts of primary, secondary, and public territory in college residence centers and offer a practical guide to assist resident students in personalizing their own spaces.

Schuh, J. H. (Ed.). *Programming and Activities in College and University Residence Halls.* Bloomington, Ind.: Association of College and University Housing Officers, 1977.

The purpose of this publication is to give residence hall personnel a systematic approach to planning residence hall programs. Several chapters deal with the programming process. A philosophical perspective toward programming is established and assessment of student needs is discussed. Contributors discuss methods to generate ideas for programs, means to involve students, and ways to evaluate. The remaining chapters provide insight into the needs of special students on modern university campuses and offer programs specifically designed to meet those needs.

Schuh, J. H., and Allen, M. R. "Implementing the Ecosystem Model." *Journal of College Student Personnel,* 1978, *19* (2), 119–122.

The authors discuss the application of the ecosystem model at Arizona State University. The areas assessed include housing, residence hall programs, health services, food services, the university police services, and the student affairs department. Redesign efforts and evaluation are described. The book includes recommendations by the planning team for expanding the project.

Scroggins, W. F., and Ivey, A. E. "Teaching and Maintaining Microcounseling Skills with a Residence Hall Staff." *Journal of College Student Personnel,* 1978, 19 (2), 158–162.

Evidence indicates that individuals trained by the microcounseling model learn helping skills quickly, maintain them over time, and produce significant changes in their clients. Pre- and posttesting on videotapes, the Personal Orientation Inventory, and the Microcounseling Skill Discrimination Index were used to investigate the effectiveness of microcounseling with student residence hall counselors at the University of Alabama. The data analysis reveals statistically significant, positive results regarding both the acquisition and maintenance of counseling skills over one year. Limitations of the study are discussed.

Stoner, K. L., and Thurman, C. W. "The Effects of Density in a Highrise Residence Hall on Helping Behavior and Social Interaction." *The Journal of College and University Student Housing,* 1978, *8* (1), 14–18.

The authors review previous research to illustrate the effects of high-density housing on the helping behaviors and social interactions of student residents. Conclusions and recommendations to overcome negative effects are provided.

Winkelpleck, J. M., and Domke, J. A. "Perceived Problems and Assistance Desired by Residence Hall Staff." *Journal of College Student Personnel,* 1977, *18* (3), 195–199.

Winkelpleck and Domke describe an empirical approach for determining residence hall staff training needs. They analyze data regarding reported frequencies of specific problems and the need for assistance by personnel across four organizational levels in three residence complexes at Iowa State University. Suggestions for using the findings, conclusions, and implications are included.

Janice L. Diehl is a residence coordinator at Kutztown State College in Kutztown, Pennsylvania. She earned a M.S. in college student personnel administration from Indiana University, Bloomington, where she was a member of the Department of Residence Life. She received a M.Ed. degree in community counseling from Lehigh University in Bethlehem, Pennsylvania, and a B.S. in Psychology from Ursinus College, Collegeville, Pennsylvania. She is a former career awareness counselor at Northhampton County Area Community College in Pennsylvania.

Index

A

Adams, C., 47
Administration, of living learning centers, 56–57
Advertising, for staff selection, 67, 75
Affirmative action, and staff selection, 67–68, 75
Aiello, J., 38, 47
Alabama, University of, microcounseling at, 109
Allen, M. R., 108
Altman, I., 41, 47, 48
American College Personnel Association (ACPA), 66, 73; Commission III, Student Residence Programs, of, 54, 104, 106
American Council on Education, 97, 99, 101
American Personnel and Guidance Association, 67
Anchors, S., 15, 21, 45, 47, 108
Anthony, V. L., 71, 78
Application blank, for staff selection, 68, 76–77
Apprenticeships, for resident assistant selection, 71, 72
Ardell, D., 26, 32
Ardrey, R., 41, 47
Arizona State University, ecosystem model at, 108
Armentrout, W., 2, 9
Astin, A. W., 31, 32, 89, 92
Atkinson, D. R., 69, 71, 78
Auburn University, environmental management at, 43, 44, 46
Aulepp, L., 82, 87, 89, 92, 93, 103, 105
Authoritarian F Scale, 72
Authority, and student involvement, 19

B

Baier, J. L., 77, 78
Bailey, L. H., 23
Bakker, C., 41, 47
Bakker-Rabdau, M., 41, 47
Ball, W. D., 71, 78
Ball State University, living learning center at, 58, 59

Bandler, R., 30n, 32
Banta, T. W., 70, 78
Baron, R., 38, 39, 41, 47
Bass, B. M., 70, 78
Bauer, G., 71, 80
Baum, A., 38, 39, 47, 49
Beatty, R. W., 66, 78
Bellucci, J. E., 103
Belmonte, A., 40, 48
Blimling, G. S., vii–ix, 1–11, 95–102, 103–104
Bloland, P., 90, 92
Bodden, J. L., 72, 78
Bradshaw, H. E., 70, 71, 79
Brady, M. V., 70, 78
Brown, R. D., 6, 8, 9, 13, 21, 29, 32, 40, 47, 52, 56, 63, 88, 92
Browning, R. C., 68, 78
Buber, M., 4, 10
Buckner, D. R., 104

C

California Personality Inventory (CPI), 71
Cannell, C. F., 69, 79
Cardozier, V., 4, 10
Carkhuff, R. R., 87, 92
Carlson, R. E., 69, 78, 79
Carnegie Council on Policy Studies in Higher Education, 95, 96, 101
Case studies, for training, 91
Casey, T. F., 68, 78
Centra, J. A., 62, 63
Chamberlain, P. C., 56, 59, 61, 62, 63, 91, 92
Change: defined, 23; strategies for, 30–31. See also Development
Chickering, A. W., 16, 17, 21, 26, 27, 28, 32, 88, 89, 92
Citrin, R. S., 29, 32
City University of New York, and economic influences, 96
Civil Rights Act of 1964, Title VII of, 67
Classes, and living learning centers, 53
Cohen, M., 1, 10
Cohen, S., 41, 48

Colesnick, L., 38, 47
College and University Environment
Scales Questionnaire, 62
Colorado State University, environment modification at, 104
Community: defined, 14; enhanced by environmental management, 46–47; and living learning centers, 58; resources on, 105
Community development: environment ideal for, 14–19; philosophy of, 13; in residence halls, 13–21; resources on, 105; student involvement in, 19–20
Connors, M., 46, 48
Contracts and selections, for living learning centers, 57–58
Conventions, and staff selection, 76
Coons, F., 16, 17, 21, 88, 92
Cooperative housing, 106
Corazzini, J. G., 84, 93, 104
Cornell University, educational programming at, 23
Correnti, R. J., 70, 71, 78
Correspondence, for staff selection, 76
Cory, W., 3, 10
Counseling, training in, 87, 88–90
Cowley, W., 6, 10
Crawley, W. J., 70, 80
Creamer, D., 104
Creed, W., 71, 79
Crookston, B. B., 14, 20, 21, 65, 78
Cross, K. P., 2, 3, 5, 10, 13–14, 16, 21, 24, 32

D

Danish, S. J., 88, 93
Davidson, A., 69, 72, 79
DeCoster, D. A., 15, 21, 52, 59, 61, 63, 83, 93, 104–105
Delozier, J., 30, 32
Delworth, U., 81, 82, 87, 89, 90, 92, 93, 103, 105, 107
Denerly, R. A., 66, 78
Development: and administrative policies and procedures, 39–40; and architectural arrangements, 37–39; areas in, 26; assessment of levels of, 27–28; defined, 23; enrichment and, 16; environmental management for, 35–49; model of programming for, 28–30; readiness for, 25; recognition of, 29; resources on, 104–105, 107–108; and territoriality, 41; theories of, 25–27;

and wellness movement, 26. *See also* Community development
Dewey, J., 2, 10
Diehl, J. L., viii, 103–109
Dolan, F. A., 71, 78
Domke, J. A., 109
Dorin, P. A., 71, 78
Dowse, E., 71, 80
Dunn, H., 26, 32
Dunnette, M. D., 69, 78
Duvall, W. J., 10, 14–15, 21

E

Economy, influences of, 96–97
Education: cognitive-affective dualism in, 4–7; and moral development, 3–4; outcomes in defining, 3–4; and residence halls, 5–6; responsibility for, 7–9
Educational programming: analysis of, 23–33; changes in, 100; goal of, 24; model for, 28–30; purpose of, 23–24; resources on, 104, 108; setting stage for, 24–25
Egan, G., 87, 93
Eigenbrod, F., 43, 47
Ender, K., 105
Enrollment: declining, 95–96; increasing, 1–2
Environment: and community development, 15–19; development through, 25, 35–49; enrichment of, 15–18; interpersonal, 15–18; normative, 18–19; physical, 15, 44–45; resources on, 104, 107; structuring of, in living learning centers, 51–64
Equal Employment Opportunity Act of 1972, 67
Equal Employment Opportunity Commission (EEOC), 67–68
Ethics, and student involvement, 19–20
Evaluation: of living learning centers, 62; and programmatic training, 90
Experimental programs, as living learning centers, 53

F

Facilities: changes in, 98–99; of living learning centers, 61
Faculty: and enrichment, 17; impact of reward system for, 2; and living learning centers, 56–57

Fair Labor Standards Act of 1963, 97
Family Educational Rights and Privacy
Act of 1974, 97
Fawcett, L., 48
Feldman, K., 3, 10, 40, 48
Flanagan, D., 105
Florida, University of, living learning
center at, 54-55
Frichette, S. R., 105-106
Funding, of living learning centers, 60

G

Galbraith, J. K., 14, 21
Garb, E., 78
Garcia, J. R., 68, 77, 79
Gaudet, F. J., 68, 78
Georgia Southwestern College, room
personalization at, 44
German, S. C., 106
Gerst, M., 38, 48
Glueck, W. F., 66, 78
Goheen, H. W., 68, 79
Government, regulation by, 97-98
Graff, R. W., 70, 71, 79
Grant, W. H., 15, 18, 21, 41, 48
Greenleaf, E., viii, 81
Greenwood, J. D., 106
Griffen, L., 47
Griggs v. *Duke Power Co.*, 67, 79
Grinder, J., 30, 32
Growth, defined, 23. *See also* Development

H

Haldane, M. B., 70, 71, 79
Hall, E., 41, 48
Hall, M., 71, 79
Hammond, E. H., 106
Hansen, W., 41, 48
Hanson, G., 66, 79
Hardee, M., 6, 10
Hauer, A. L., 88, 93
Heilweil, M., 36, 48
Hennessy, T. J., vii, 13-21
Hettler, B., 26, 27, 28, 32
High, T., 38, 48
Higher education: as change agent, 24;
and cognitive development, 2-3;
compartmentalization of, 1-3; demo-
cratic process in, 18-19; described, 1;
influences on, 95-98; myths about,
18. *See also* Institutions

Holahan, C., 39, 48
Holbrook, D., 3, 10
Holland, J., 40, 48
Hoyt, D. P., 69, 72, 79
Huebner, L., 89, 93
Human relations, training in, 86-88
Humanities, and enrichment, 16-17
Hurst, J. C., 6-7, 10, 107
Huxley, T., 4, 10

I

Illinois, University of, living learning
center at, 55-56, 57, 59, 61
Indiana University, living learning cen-
ter at, 55, 56, 57, 59, 60-61
Inkeles, A., 14, 21
Institutions: living learning center rela-
tionship with, 59-60; perspective of,
toward resident assistants, 83
Interpersonal Process Recall, 87, 103
Interviews, for staff selection, 67-68,
69, 77
Iowa State University, staff training
needs at, 109
Ivey, A. E., 87, 93, 108

J

Jackson, G., 47, 48
Jackson, S., 15, 21, 45, 47, 108
Jencks, C., 17, 18, 21
Job analysis, for staff selection, 66, 75-
76
Jones, J. E., 91, 93
Jung, C., 42

K

Kagan, N., 87, 93, 103
Kahn, R. L., 69, 79
Kalsbeek, D., 43, 48
Kane, N., 105
Katz, J., 2, 10
Kipp, D. J., 71, 79

L

Leaderless group discussion, for resi-
dent assistant selection, 70, 72
Leafgren, F., vii-viii, 23-33
Lembcke, B., 106
Lifestyle Assessment Questionnaire, 27
Like-major units, as living learning cen-
ters, 52-53

Living learning centers: analysis of, 51–64; components of, 55–62; defined, 54–55; philosophical bases for, 51–52; resource on, 107; size of, 58–59; structures for, 52–53
Lopez, F. M., Jr., 66, 68, 79

M

Mable, P., 7, 10, 14–15, 21, 52, 59, 61, 63, 83, 93, 104–105
McConnel, T., 1, 7, 10
McCormick, J. E., 70, 78
McLaughlin, G., 48
Magnarella, P. J., 58, 59, 61, 62, 63, 106
Malone, D., 43, 48
Mandel, D., 47
Mandell, M. M., 68, 79
March, G., 1, 10
Mayfield, E. C., 69, 78, 79
Meade, C. J., 86, 87, 88, 93
Mehrabian, A., 41, 48
Michigan, University of, living learning center at, 55, 58, 59
Microcounseling, as training model, 87, 108–109
Microcounseling Skill Discrimination Index, 109
Mill, J. S., 20, 21
Miller, T. K., 3, 6, 7, 10, 17, 21, 25, 27, 33, 56, 63, 88, 93
Milterberger, L., 103–104
Miner, J. B., 66, 68, 69, 76, 79
Miner, M. G., 68, 76, 79
Minetti, R. H., 73, 79
Mitchell, K. N., 69, 80
Montagu, A., 4, 5, 10
Montgomery, J., 35, 48
Moore, M., 90, 93, 107
Moos, R. H., 38, 40, 107
Morrill, W. H., 107
Morton, L. J., 71, 79
Mosel, J. N., 68, 79
Mullozzi, A., Jr., 70, 71, 79
Murphy, F., 96, 102
Murphy, R., 8, 10
Myers, I., 42, 48
Myers-Briggs Type Indicator (MBTI), 42–44, 71

N

Nair, D. A., 70, 79
National Association for Women Deans, Administrators, and Counselors, 73

National Association of Student Personnel Administrators, 73
National Center for Education Statistics, 1, 10
National Orientation Directors Association, 90
Nebraska, University of, living learning center at, 61
Neuro-Linguistic Programming, 30–31
Newcomb, T., 3, 10, 40, 48
Newman, O., 45, 46, 48
Norms, criteria for establishing, 20–21
Northern Illinois University, educational programming at, 104
Northwestern University, living learning center at, 58

O

O'Donnell, W. J., 107
O'Leary, L. R., 66, 79
Oetting, E. R., 107
Oglesby, C. L., 107
Ohio State University, matching suitemates at, 43
Operational services, training in, 83–84
Ostroth, D. D., viii, 65–80

P

Parker, C., 107
Pedigo, E., 48
Peer ratings, for resident assistant selection, 70
Peres, S. H., 68, 77, 79
Personal Orientation Inventory (POI), 71, 109
Peterson, D. A., 78
Pfeiffer, J. U., 91, 93
Philosophy, of living learning center, 51–52, 55–56
Planning: for staff selection, 75; of training, 82–83
Plumbley, P. R., 66, 78
Powell, J. R., 81, 83, 93
Prince, J. S., 3, 6, 7, 10, 17, 21, 25, 27, 33, 56, 63, 88, 93
Programming: of living learning centers, 59; training in, 88–90. *See also* Educational programming

R

References, written, for staff selection, 68, 77

Rehabilitation Act of 1973, Section 504 of, 97

Reilley, R. R., 62, 64

Research, need for, 99–100

Residence halls: administrative policies and procedures for, 39–40; architectural arrangements of, 37–39; changes predicted for, 98–101; community development in, 13–21; corridor arrangement of, 38; damage and vandalism reduction in, 45–46; dissatisfaction with, 35–36; educational programming in, 7–8, 23–33; educational responsibilities of, 7–9; environmental management of, 35–49; history of, vii, 5–6; as living learning centers, 51–64; lounges of, 38, 45–46; overcrowding of, 39, 109; personalized, 44–45; predictions about, 98; privacy and solitude in, 45, 98; recommendations for, 101; resident assistant training for, 81–93; resources on, 103–109; role of, 1–11; staff selection for, 65–80; suite arrangements of, 38; theoretical framework for improving, 40–42

Resident assistants (RAs): second-and third-year, 83; selection of, 69–72, 106; training for, 81–93

Residential colleges, as living learning centers, 53

Resumé, for staff selection, 68, 76–77

Rickgarn, R. L., 91, 93

Riesman, D., 17, 18, 21

Riker, H. C., 9, 10, 15, 21, 52, 63–64

Rim, Y., 68, 79

Roethke, T., 18

Role playing, for resident assistant selection, 70

Roommates, matching, 42–43

Rowe, L. P., viii, 51–64, 100

Rudolph, F., 14, 21

Russell, J., 41, 48

S

St. Clair, T., 4, 10

Sanford, N., 3, 10, 23, 24, 25, 33, 40, 48

Satir, V., 30n, 32

Schneider, B., 66, 68, 69, 80

Schneier, C. E., 66, 78

Schroeder, C. C., viii, 15, 21, 35–49, 70, 71, 80, 100, 107–108

Schroeder, P., 71, 80

Schuh, J. H., vii–ix, 7, 11, 62, 64, 81–93, 95–102, 108

Scriven, M., 19, 20, 21

Scroggins, W. F., 108

Selection of staff: and affirmative action, 67–68, 75; analysis of, 65–80; defined, 66; interviews for, 67–68, 69, 77; procedure reliability and validity in, 68–69; procedures used in, 74–75; of professionals, 72–75; recommendations for, 75–76; of resident assistants, 69–72; steps in, 66–67; techniques for, 76–77

Shaffer, R. H., 106

Shay, J., 6, 11

Sheeder, W. B., 70, 80

Shelton, J. L., 84, 93

Sherrod, D., 41, 48

Simon, P., 2, 11, 96, 102

Social climate, environmental management of, 40, 41, 42–44

Sommer, R., 44, 48

Sonders, O. L., 70, 79

Special interest units, as living learning centers, 52

Spees, E. R., 70, 71, 79

Staff: as change agents, 27–28, 29; changes in, 99; competencies desired for, 65, 73–74; development process for, 27; of living learning centers, 60–61; manual for, 85, 91; qualifications of, 8–9; roles and functions of, 35; selection of, 65–80

Stamatakos, B., 4, 11

Stamatakos, L., 4, 8, 11

Stern, G., 1, 11

Stoner, K. L., 109

Strohm, M., 105

Stroup, H., 6, 11

Structure, and student involvement, 19

Student Development Task Inventory, 27

Student services: lateral communication by, 7; legal issues in, 106–107; professionals in, 6–7; theories of, 6

Student-environment congruence, management of, 40–41, 42, 44

Students: characteristics of, 58–59, 97; individual needs of, 37; involvement of, in community development, 19–20. See also Development

Suitemates, matching, 43

Sundstrom, E., 38, 48

Support services, training in, 84–86
Sweetwood, H., 38, 48
Syracuse University, living learning center at, 57–58

T

Taylor, V. R., 69, 80
Team building, and training, 90–91
Territoriality: management of, 41, 42, 45–46; resources on, 108
Terry, M., 10, 14–15, 21
Tests, standardized, for resident assistant selection, 71–72
Thayer, P. W., 78
Thurman, C. W., 109
Tibbits, S., 70, 80
Titus, C., 40, 49
Tollefson, A., 6, 11
Training of resident assistants: analysis of, 81–93; in human relations, 86–88; issues in, 90–92; in operations, 83–84; planning of, 82–83; in programming/advising, 88–90; resource people for, 88; resources on, 103–104, 105, 107, 109; in sequential skills, 82–83; in support services, 84–86
Travis, J., 26, 33
Truitt, J., 3, 4, 11
Trumbo, D., 69, 80
Tuttle, C. E., 70, 71, 78

U

Ulrich, L., 69, 80

V

Valins, S., 39, 49
Van Hecke, C. E., 90, 93
Vermont, University of, living learning center at, 55, 57, 58, 59–69, 61, 107

W

Wachowiak, D., 71, 80
Wagoner, D., 18
Walsh, W. B., 72, 78
Ward, S., 48
Warner, R., 43, 46, 48, 49
Webster, E. C., 67, 69, 80
Wellness: defined, 26; educational programming for, 31
Werner, W. L., 91, 92
West, N., 46, 49
Wilcox, B., 39, 48
William and Mary, College of, living learning center at, 57, 58, 59
Williams, D. E., 62, 64
Williams, T. D., 78
Willis, B. S., 70, 71, 80
Wilson, S., 104
Winkelpleck, J. M., 109
Winston, R., 27, 33
Wisconsin, University of, Stevens Point, physical development program at, 31
Wohlwill, J., 41, 49
Wotruba, R. T., 70, 80
Wyrick, T. J., 69, 80

Y

Yarris, E., 81, 93

New Directions Quarterly Sourcebooks

New Directions for Student Services is one of several distinct series of quarterly sourcebooks published by Jossey-Bass. The sourcebooks in each series are designed to serve both as *convenient compendiums* of the latest knowledge and practical experience on their topics and as *long-life reference tools.*

One-year, four-sourcebook subscriptions for each series cost $18 for individuals (when paid by personal check) and $30 for institutions, libraries, and agencies. Single copies of earlier sourcebooks are available at $6.95 each *prepaid* (or $7.95 each when *billed*).

A complete listing is given below of current and past sourcebooks in the *New Directions for Student Services* series. The titles and editors-in-chief of the other series are also listed. To subscribe, or to receive further information, write: New Directions Subscriptions, Jossey-Bass Inc., Publishers, 433 California Street, San Francisco, California 94104.

New Directions for Student Services
Ursula Delworth and Gary R. Hanson, Editors-in-Chief
1978:   1. *Evaluating Program Effectiveness,* Gary R. Hanson
        2. *Training Competent Staff,* Ursula Delworth
        3. *Reducing the Dropout Rate,* Lee Noel
        4. *Applying New Developmental Findings,* Lee Knefelkamp, Carole Widick, Clyde A. Parker
1979:   5. *Consulting on Campus,* M. Kathryn Hamilton, Charles J. Meade
        6. *Utilizing Futures Research,* Frederick R. Brodzinski
        7. *Establishing Effective Programs,* Margaret J. Barr, Lou Ann Keating
        8. *Redesigning Campus Environments,* Lois Huebner
1980:   9. *Applying Management Techniques,* Cecelia H. Foxley
     10. *Serving Handicapped Students,* Hazel Z. Sprandel, Marlin R. Schmidt
     11. *Providing Student Services for the Adult Learner,* Arthur Shriberg
     12. *Responding to Changes in Financial Aid Programs,* Shirley F. Binder

New Directions for Child Development
William Damon, Editor-in-Chief

New Directions for College Learning Assistance
Kurt V. Lauridsen, Editor-in-Chief

New Directions for Community Colleges
Arthur M. Cohen, Editor-in-Chief
Florence B. Brawer, Associate Editor

New Directions for Continuing Education
Alan B. Knox, Editor-in-Chief

New Directions for Exceptional Children
James J. Gallagher, Editor-in-Chief

New Directions for Experiential Learning
Pamela J. Tate, Editor-in-Chief
Morris T. Keeton, Consulting Editor

New Directions for Higher Education
JB Lon Hefferlin, Editor-in-Chief

New Directions for Institutional Advancement
A. Westley Rowland, Editor-in-Chief

New Directions for Institutional Research
Marvin W. Peterson, Editor-in-Chief

New Directions for Mental Health Services
H. Richard Lamb, Editor-in-Chief

New Directions for Methodology of Social and Behavioral Science
Donald W. Fiske, Editor-in-Chief

New Directions for Program Evaluation
Scarvia B. Anderson, Editor-in-Chief

New Directions for Teaching and Learning
Kenneth E. Eble and John F. Noonan, Editors-in-Chief

New Directions for Testing and Measurement
William B. Schrader, Editor-in-Chief